The Classic Collection of Chinese Ancient Calligraphy

中國古代書法經典精粹

Shiwen Tao 陶詩文　Commentary 评注

Publisher： iCultures Publicatioins　　　Editor in Chief 主編　Hui Pang 龐輝

The Classic Collection of Ancient Chinese Calligraphy
中國古代書法經典精粹

Commentary 评注：陶詩文　Shiwen Tao

Editor in Chief 主編：　Hui Pang 龐輝
Executive Editor 責任編輯：Phoenix Huan
Art Design 美術設計：　Minxu Tang 唐民旭
Translate 翻譯：　Huilin Yu
Translation Review 翻譯審核：　Qi Li

ISBN / 國際標準書號：9798987135327
LCCN / 美國圖書館編目號碼：2023906584

Publisher 出版商：　iCultures Publicatioins 美國文化橋出版社

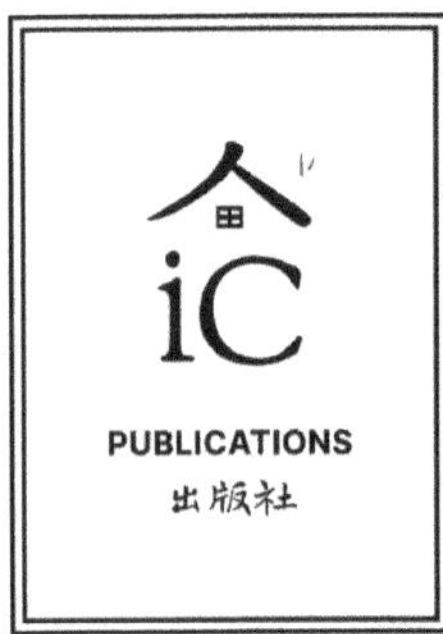

仰望經典
Admire The Classics

陶詩文

　　春有百花秋有月，夏有涼風冬有雪，時節變換播散出異樣的美意，時空的挪移誕生無盡芳華，在天宇之間的華夏大地上書法藝術猶如一朵雪雪奇葩獨一無二地綻放於世界藝林之中，彰顯著中華燦爛瑰麗的古代文明，耀眼著無盡的藝術光輝和魅力。回尋中華幾千年書法藝術發展的軌跡墨痕，望見無數文人騷客、王侯將相、名流豪士、云云百姓行走其間，抒懷心意，揮筆人生；徜徉在那豐沛浩瀚的書法藝術塊寶之中，那變幻莫測的線條猶如脫韁駿馬揚蹄而來絕塵而去，那飄若浮雲，矯若驚龍的態勢無不讓學輩們為之傾倒陶醉；鐵書銀鉤，冠絕古今的書法經典引無數後學為之仰望。

　　中華書法藝術源遠流長，書體沿革流變過程一路華彩迷人，芳香四溢。先秦用筆、結體和章法已見雛形；兩漢魏晉書寫出了漢字的美感和筆意，書聖王羲之書下了草書的典範；唐代楷書確立了“楷模”之法，登峰造極；宋元書法帖學流行，個性張揚十足；明代文人書法揮灑情感、一任心靈，獨具創新；清代碑學博興，借古開今，流派紛呈。

　　王羲之顏真卿等大書家自當仰望，虔誠膜拜，但由於他們作品出版甚眾，故本書未作緝納。本書特精選出版甚少資料難尋的中國古代二十一位經典名家劉環之、張冀、向秀、陸機、王珣、王薈、王操之、王煥之、王廞、王導、王珣、王濛、王洽、王彬、王徽之、狄仁傑、虞世南、歐陽詢、褚遂良、韓愈、李德裕之書已飧讀者，讓我們一起仰望經典，向經典致敬！

Admire The Classics

Shiwen Tao

Spring brings forth hundreds of flowers, while autumn brings the moon; summer brings cool breezes, and winter brings snow. As the seasons change, they bring out unique beauty, and the passage of time gives birth to endless splendor.

In the vast land of China, calligraphy is like a unique and exquisite flower, blossoming in the world of art, showcasing the splendid ancient civilization of China, radiating endless artistic brilliance and charm.

Looking back at the trajectory of calligraphy art in China for thousands of years, we see countless literati, nobles, celebrities, and ordinary people expressing their feelings, writing down their life experiences with their pens.

As we immerse ourselves in the abundant and magnificent treasures of calligraphy art, the ever-changing lines are like untamed horses galloping away in a cloud of dust, their graceful and powerful posture leaving viewers enthralled and intoxicated.

The classic calligraphy works that have stood the test of time and surpassed all others are revered and worshipped by many, including the great calligraphers such as Wang Xizhi and Yan Zhenqing. However, due to the abundance of their published works, they are not included in this book.

This book carefully selects the works of twenty-one classic Chinese calligraphy masters, such as Liu Huanzhi, Zhang Ji, Xiang Xiu, Lu Ji, Wang Min, Wang Hui, Wang Caozhi, Wang Huanzhi, Wang Xin, Wang Dao, Wang Xun, Wang Meng, Wang Qia, Wang Bin, Wang Huizhi, Di Renjie, Yu Shinan, Chu Suiliang, Han Yu, and Li Deyu. These works are rarely published and difficult to find, and we present them to the readers as a way to admire and pay tribute to the classics!

卷首語

劉環之（生卒年不詳），字元寶。"善行草八分書，二王之次，骨力全，軌範宏麗。"

張翼（生卒年不詳），字君祖。真書學鍾繇，草書學王羲之，皆能精妙。南朝宋羊欣稱其："善學人書，寫羲之表，表出，經日不覺，後雲'幾欲亂真'。"

向秀（約二二七----二七二），字子期。魏晉竹林七賢之一。向秀喜談老莊之學，曾注《莊子》，注未成便過世，郭象承其《莊子》餘緒，成書《莊子注》三十三篇。另著有《思舊賦》《難嵇叔夜養生論》。其書法"有拔俗之韻"，任性不羈，得之自然，清神逸氣。

陸機（二六一---三〇三），字士衡。用筆古雅，點畫蒼勁有力，樸實雄厚。筆劃短促有力，流露出古雅蒼勁的風致，短促渾厚，骨力充盈。筆法圓渾，"筆力堅勁倔強，如萬歲枯藤。"

王珉（三五一----三八八），字季琰。善行書，時人言其"嘗書四正秦，白朝操筆，至暮便竟。首尾如一，又無誤字。"其書法"露鋒而豁懷，傍禮樂而無檢，猶搏扶搖而坐致，超峻極而非險"。

王薈（四六四---五四九，字敬文。宋代陳思《書小史》稱其："善行書。"其書法筆鋒剛健挺拔，極有力度，神韻清和秀雅，筆力斬截，筆鋒挺秀，獨具一格，與其恬虛守清、不競榮利的人品相近。

王操之（生卒年不詳），字子重，王羲之之子。擅長草隸，其筆法舒緩自然，不作大的起伏與頓挫，棱角泯滅而使轉精美。黃伯思《東觀餘論》雲："王氏凝、操、徽、渙之四子書，與子敬書俱傳，皆得家範，而體各不同。操之得其體。"

王廞（生卒年不詳），字伯輿，東晉後期政治人物、書法家。擅長書法，善行書。唐人評價其作品："溫溫伯輿，亦扇其風。風流之表，軒冕之中。骨體慢正，精彩沖融。已高天然，恨乏其功。如承奕葉之貴冑，備夙訓之神童。"

王渙之（生卒年不詳），字子高，王羲之第四子。自幼學習書法，善行草書。黃伯思《東觀餘論》雲："王氏凝、操、徽、渙之四子書，與子敬書俱傳，皆得家範，而體各不同。渙之得其貌。"參加了傳譽千古的蘭亭聚會。

王導（二七六 --- 三三九），字茂弘，小字阿龍。學習鍾繇，衛瓘之法，而能自成一格，其書法"飽含風骨卻又典雅高韻，不僅有武將的魄勇，也不失戲魚般的靈動"。唐代竇臮評曰："將以潤色前範，遺芳後車，風棱載蓄，高利有餘。"

王珣（三四九 ---- 四〇〇），字元琳，小字法護。王珣工書法，董其昌評其書法："王珣瀟灑古澹，東晉風流，宛然在眼。"其書"如升初日，如清風，如雲如霞，如煙，如幽林曲洞"的晉人韻味。

王濛（三〇九 --- 三四七），字仲祖，小字阿奴。王濛擅隸書和章草。《述書賦》評"仲祖慕元常之則，結束體正，肆力專成，猶棟樑富於合抱，巧匠斫而未精。"黃庭堅雲："觀王濛書，想見其人秀整，幾所謂毫髮無遺恨者。"

王洽（三二三 --- 三五八），字敬和。王羲之說："弟書遂不減吾。"李嗣真《書品後》評論他說："體裁用筆，全似逸少，虛薄不住。"其書有"乘風之勢，卓然孤秀，麗雅有韻。"

王彬（二七八 --- 三三六），字世儒。東晉初年權臣王敦和王導的堂弟，荊州刺史王廙的弟弟。東晉建立後，王彬逐步升遷，官至侍中。其草書筆走龍蛇，飄若浮雲，神采動人。

王徽之（三三八 ---- 三八六），字子猷，王羲之第五子。其書法長於行草，以韻勝，揮灑自如，筆法多變，妍美流暢。宋《宣和書譜》評其書法"作字亦自韻勝"。

狄仁傑（六三〇 -- 七〇〇），字懷英。善書法，與歐陽詢、褚遂良、薛稷合稱"初唐四大家。"其書法"筆意婉厚，結體端雅，中宮密切，氣象峻整。"

虞世南（五五八 -- 六三八），字伯施。《書斷》稱其書"得大令（王獻之）之宏規，含五方之正色，姿榮秀出，智勇存焉。秀嶺危峰，處處間起；行草之際，尤所偏工。及其暮齒，加以遒逸。"

歐陽詢（五五七 -- 六四一），字信本。後人以其書於平正中見險絕，最便初學，號為"歐體"。唐張懷瓘《書斷》："詢八體盡能，筆力險勁，篆體尤精，飛白冠絕，峻於古人，猶龍蛇戰鬥之象，雲霧輕寵之勢，風旋雷激，操舉若神。"

褚遂良（五九六 -- 六五九），字登善。褚遂良工書法，初學虞世南，後取法王羲之。魏征贊曰："褚遂良下筆遒勁，甚得王逸少體。"蘇軾評曰："骨氣深穩，體兼眾妙，精能之至，反造疏淡。"

韓愈（七六八 -- 八二四），字退之。唐代文學家、哲學家、思想家。宋朱長文《續書斷》雲："退之雖不學書，而天骨勁健，自有高處，非眾人所及。"

李德裕（七八七 -- 八五〇），字文饒。唐代文學家、政治家、書法家。近代學者羅振玉十分推崇李德裕的書法，以為唐人隸書"尚存古法者，有唐惟李衛公一人耳。"

Preface

Liu Huanzhi (birth and death unknown), with the courtesy name of Yuanbao. "He was good at writing in the style of the Eight-Part Cursive Script, second only to the Two Wang, with full strength and grand style."

Zhang Yi (birth and death unknown), with the courtesy name of Junzu, was a master of calligraphy in both regular and cursive script, following the styles of Zhong Yao and Wang Xizhi, respectively. The Southern Song Dynasty's Yang Xin praised him: "He was a good learner of calligraphy, writing in the style of Wang Xizhi, and his works were so exquisite that one could not tell the difference between them and the originals."

Xiang Xiu (about 227-272AD), also known as Zi Qi, was one of the Seven Sages of the Bamboo Grove in the Wei and Jin Dynasties. He was fond of Lao Tzu's teachings and had annotated the Zhuangzi before his death. Guo Xiang took over the unfinished Zhuangzi annotation and completed it in thirty-three chapters. He also wrote the ""Ode to the Past"" and the "Refute Ji Shuye's Theory of Health Preservation." His calligraphy had a unique charm and was unrestrained and natural, with a clear and elegant spirit.

Lu Ji (261-303AD), whose style name was Shiheng. His calligraphy is elegant and vigorous, simple and powerful. His strokes are short and powerful, revealing an elegant and vigorous style, short and powerful, full of strength. His strokes are round and thick, "the strength of his brush is strong and stubborn, like a withered vine of ten thousand years."

Wang Min (351-388AD), with the style name Ji Yan, was good at calligraphy. People at the time said of him, "He could write four scrolls of Qin script in one day, from morning to night, without any mistakes from beginning to end. His calligraphy was bold and unrestrained, with no hint of formality, promptly ascend and descend, surpass limits and danger "

Wang Hui (464 – 549AD), Zi Jingwen. Chen Si of the Song Dynasty called him "good at writing" in his 《The Book of Little History of Calligraphy》. His calligraphy was bold and vigorous, with great strength, precise and elegant charm, cutting strokes, sharp and elegant, unique, and similar to his humble, non-competitive, and non-profitable character.

Wang Caozhi (birth and death unknown), also known as Zi Chong, is the son of Wang Xizhi. He was skilled in grass-style calligraphy, with a gentle and natural style, without significant ups and downs and jerks, corners blurred and transformed into exquisite beauty. Huang Bosi "Eastern View Extra Lecture," said: "The four characters of Wang's family, Ning, Cao, Hui, and Huan, were passed on together with Zi Jing's book, all conforming to the family style, but each having its style. Cao inherited his father's calligraphy skills."

Wang Xin (birth and death unknown), also known as Bo Yu, was a political figure and calligrapher in the late Eastern Jin Dynasty. Skilled at calligraphy, he was praised for his works by the Tang people: "Bo Yu's calligraphy style is gentle and graceful, with elegance, advanced technique, rigorous and exquisite, brilliant and wise."

Wang Huanzhi (birth and death unknown), also known as Zigao, was the fourth son of Wang Xizhi. Since his childhood, he studied calligraphy and was skilled in cursive scripts. According to Huang Bosi's "Eastern View of Yu Theory," "The four sons of the Wang family, Ning, Cao, Hui and Huan, all inherited the family style, but with different styles. Huan's calligraphy is distinctive." He also participated in the famous Lan Ting gathering.

Wang Dao (276-339AD), with the courtesy name Maohong and the pseudonym A-Long, studied the calligraphy of Zhong Yao and Wei Guan and was able to create his style. His calligraphy "is full of vigor yet elegant and graceful, with not only the boldness of a warrior but also the agility of a fish." Dou Ji of the Tang Dynasty commented on: " He embellishes and refines the tradition of past masters, leaving behind a lasting legacy. His strokes are sharp and precise yet contain a richness and depth that showcase his exceptional skill.'"

Wang Xun (349-400 AD), with the courtesy name Yuanlin and the pseudonym Fahua, was a skilled calligrapher of the Eastern Jin Dynasty. Dong Qichang praised his calligraphy, saying "Wang Xun is both unconstrained and ancient, with the elegance and grace of the Eastern Jin, his calligraphy is like the rising sun, a clear breeze, clouds and mist, smoke, and the winding paths of a secluded forest," embodying the style of the Jin Dynasty.

Wang Meng (309-347AD), whose courtesy name is Zhongzu and nickname is Anu, was skilled in the regular script and cursive script. The "A poetic description of calligraphic art." commented on him, "Zhongzu pays homage to Yuan Changzhi's principle, finishing his body uprightly, being proficient in concentration, resembling beams and rafters that are richly combined, and carpenters who are skillful but not refined." Huang Tingjian said, "Observing Wang Meng's calligraphy, one can imagine his elegant and neat character. It is as if there are no regrets in his pursuit of perfection in his art, leaving no hair's breadth unattended."

Wang Qia (323-358AD), with the courtesy name Jinghe. Wang Xizhi said of him, "My younger brother's calligraphy is not inferior to mine." Li Si Zhen commented on " Book Reviewing " saying: "his style and brushwork resemble those of Yishao(王羲之), his work is ethereal and weightless but never insubstantial." His calligraphy is said to possess "a unique and outstanding elegance, refined and graceful with a sense of rhythm."

Wang Bin (278-336AD), courtesy name Shiru, was a cousin of the influential minister's Wang Dun and Wang Dao in the early period of the Eastern Jin Dynasty and the younger brother of Wang Yi, the governor of Jingzhou. After establishing the Eastern Jin Dynasty, Wang Bin gradually rose in rank and eventually became a courtier. His cursive script was full of dragon and snake-like curves and had a grace and elegance that moved people.

Wang Huizhi (338-386AD), courtesy name Ziyou, was the fifth son of Wang Xizhi. He excelled at the cursive script, with a mastery of rhyme, a natural fluidity, and a versatility in brushwork. The Song Dynasty's "Xuanhe Book Catalogue" praised his calligraphy as having "a natural sense of rhyme in his writing."

Di Renjie (630-700AD), also known as Huaiying, was a famous calligrapher in ancient China. Along with Ouyang Xun, Chu Suiliang, and Xue Ji, he was one of the "Four Great Calligraphers of the Early Tang Dynasty." His calligraphy is known for its graceful and robust strokes, elegant structure, dense and connected center strokes, and strong and balanced overall composition.

Yu Shinan (558-638AD), also known as Boshi, was a famous calligrapher in ancient China. According to " Book of Evaluating Calligraphers" , his calligraphy was described as "having the grandeur of Wang Xizhi's calligraphy, incorporating the essence of calligraphy from all five directions, with a beautiful and magnificent style, and showing both wisdom and courage. His regular script is like the beautiful and lofty mountains, and his cursive script is particularly distinctive with his own personal style. Even in his later years, his calligraphy remained strong and powerful."

Ouyang Xun (557-641AD), also known as Xinben, was a famous calligrapher in ancient China. His calligraphy is characterized by its combination of stability and danger, making it very suitable for beginners. His style is therefore known as the "Ou Style" (欧 体). Zhang Huaiyi, a Tang Dynasty scholar, once described Ouyang Xun's calligraphy in "Book of Evaluating Calligraphers" : " His execution of the eight styles was masterful, his brushwork bold and vigorous, and his seal script particularly exquisite. His flying white style surpassed all others and his calligraphy was as imposing as the battle between dragons and snakes, yet as tender as the gentle embrace of clouds and mist. His movements were swift and powerful, as if executed by a divine being."

Chu Suiliang (596-659AD), with the courtesy name of Dengshan, was a skilled calligrapher who initially studied under Yu Shinan and later drew inspiration from the style of Wang Xizhi. Wei Zheng praised Chu's calligraphy, saying that "his brushwork is powerful and vigorous, very much in line with the style of Wang Yi Shao (i.e., Wang Xizhi)." Meanwhile, Su Shi commented that "his calligraphy has deep and steady bones, combines various subtleties, reaches the pinnacle of precision and skill, and yet appears free and unstrained."

Han Yu (768-824AD), also known as Tui Zhi, was a Tang Dynasty literary figure, philosopher, and thinker. The Song Dynasty writer Zhu Changwen wrote in his book ' Continuation of Evaluating Calligraphers':" Although Han Yu did not study books, he possessed a strong and vigorous temperament that was innate to him. Through his own efforts, he achieved unique accomplishments that were beyond the reach of most people. "

Li Deyu (787-850AD), courtesy name Wenrao, was a Tang dynasty literary figure, politician, and calligrapher. Modern scholar Luo Zhenyu highly praised Li Deyu's calligraphy, stating that "among the surviving ancient methods of clerical script, only Li Weigong (Li Deyu) from the Tang dynasty is outstanding."

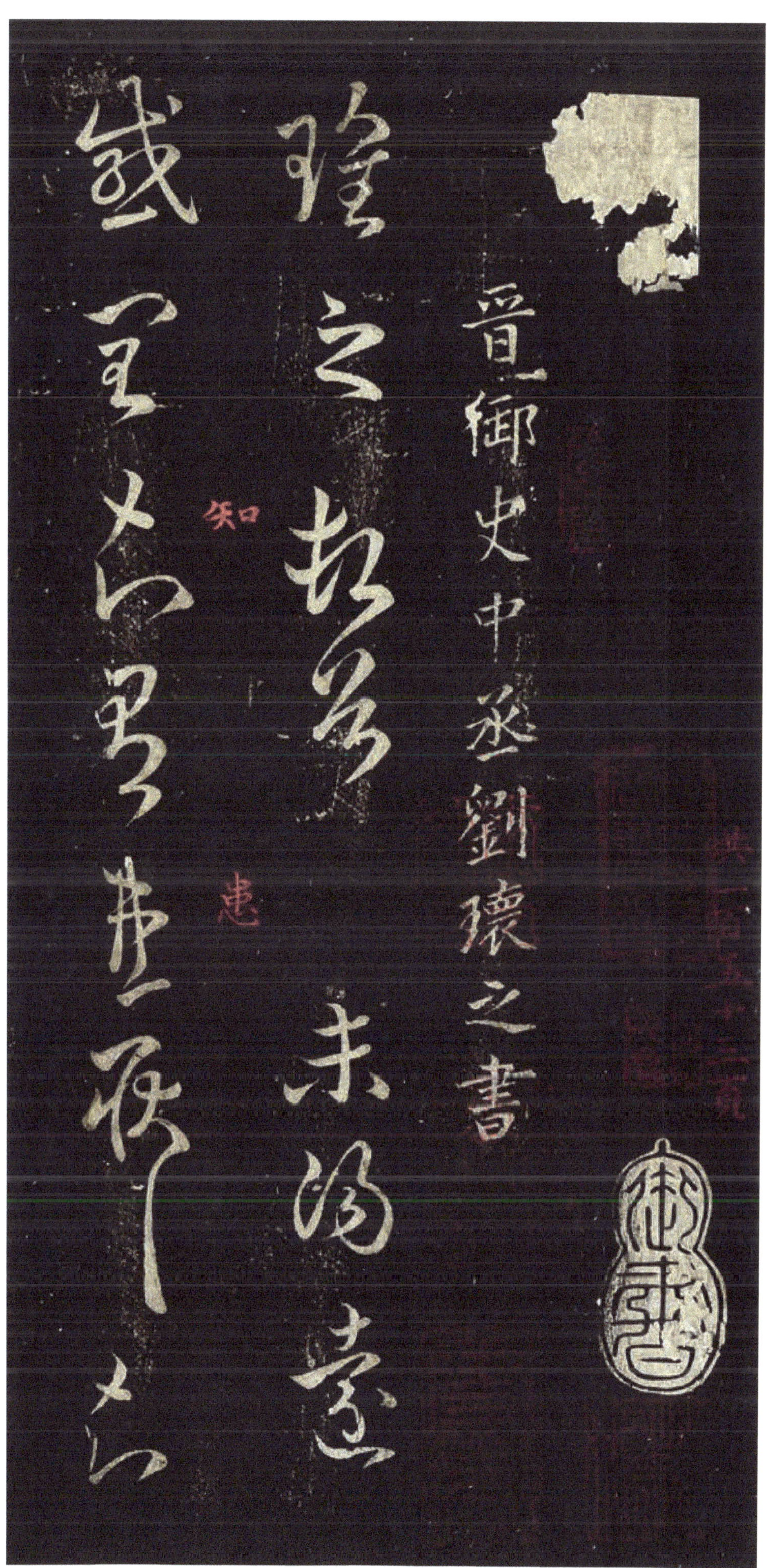
晉御史中丞劉瓌之書

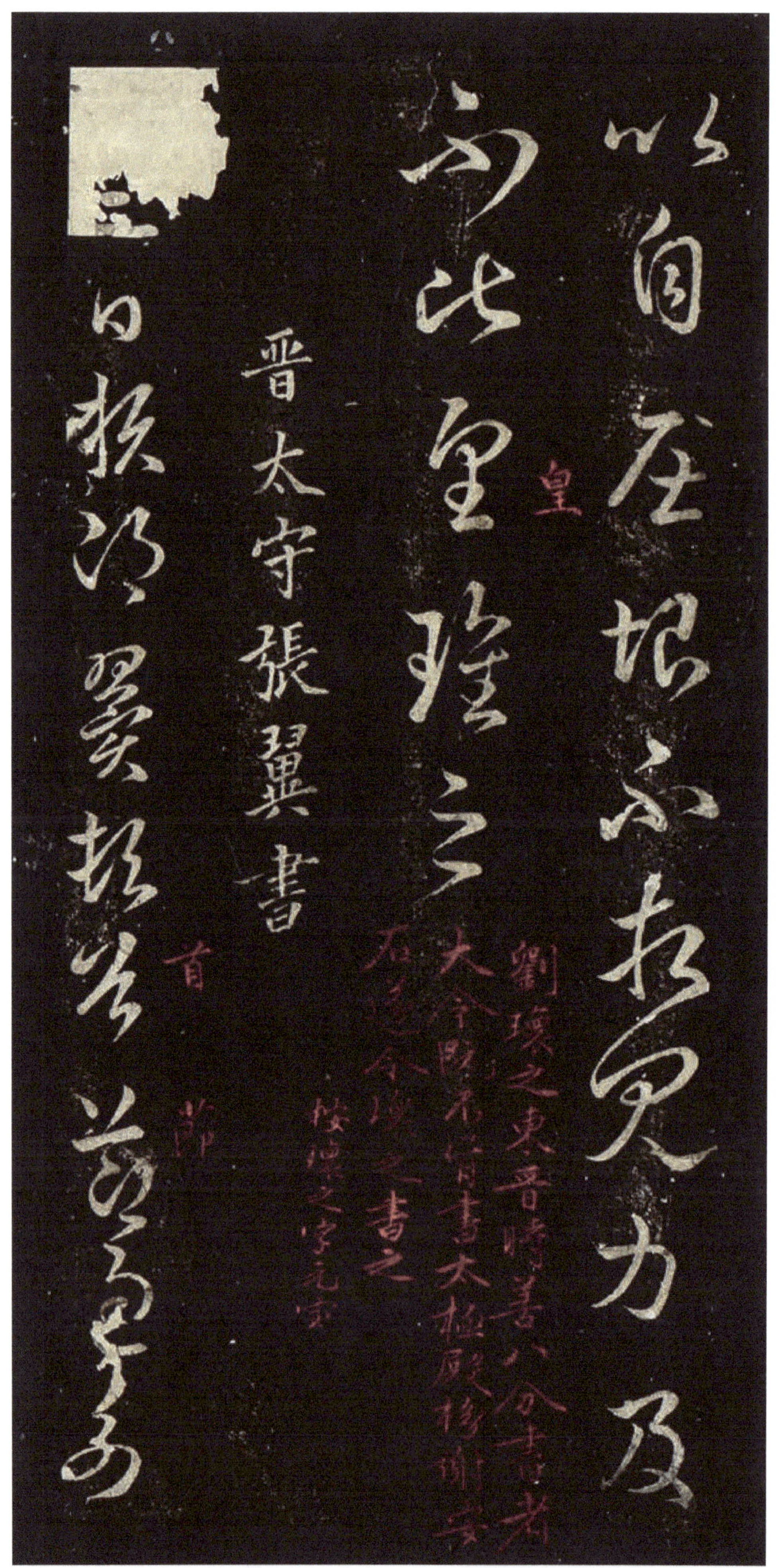

晉太守張翼書
皇
劉瓌之東晉時善八分書者
大字陽不可得書之太極殿榜題
石乃不可得而書之
按瓌之字元云
百節

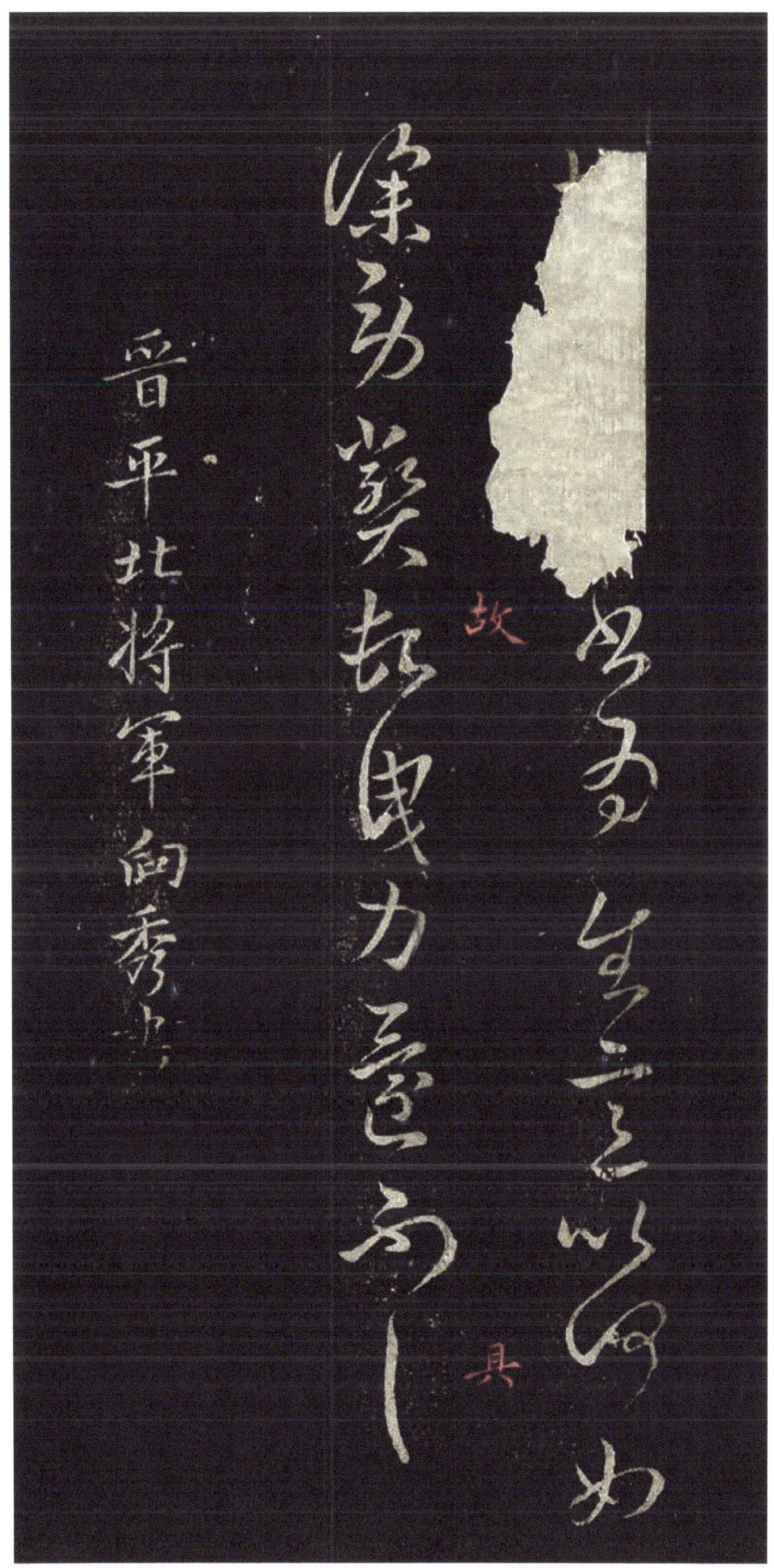
故
具
晉平北將軍向秀少

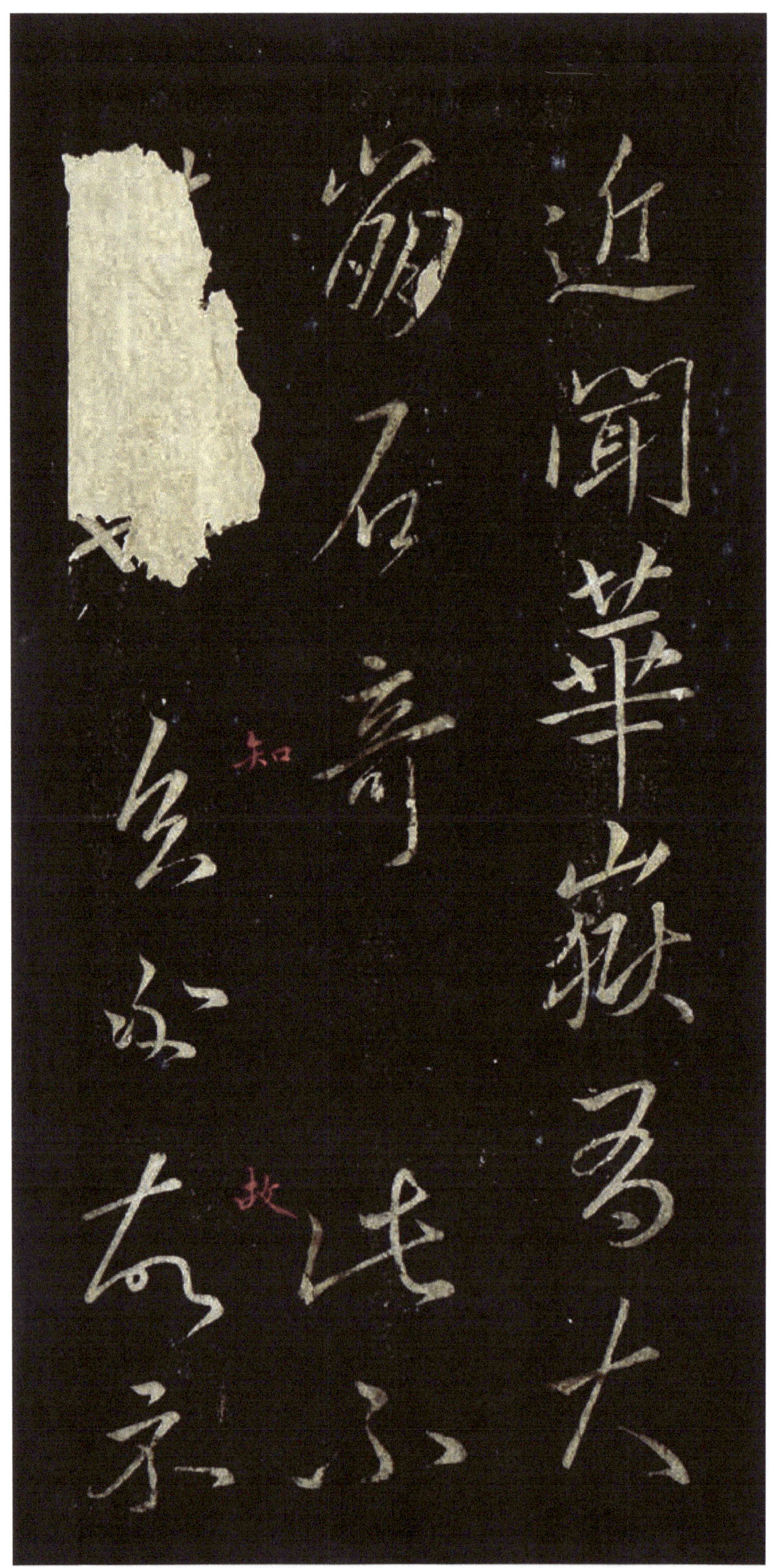

近聞華嶽多
崩石齊
知
氣
故
此
大
不
不

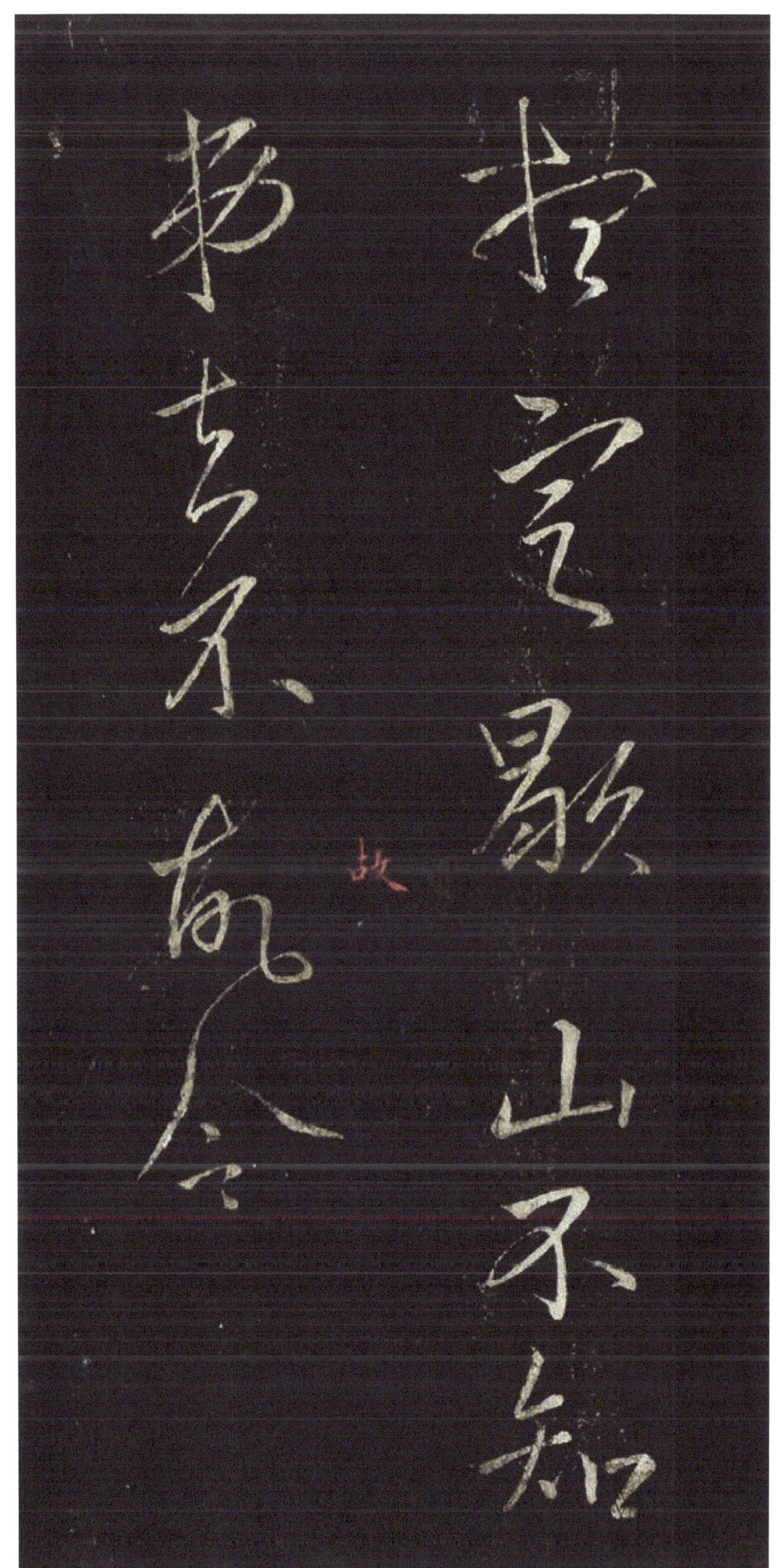
松竟歌山不知
書去不風人今
故

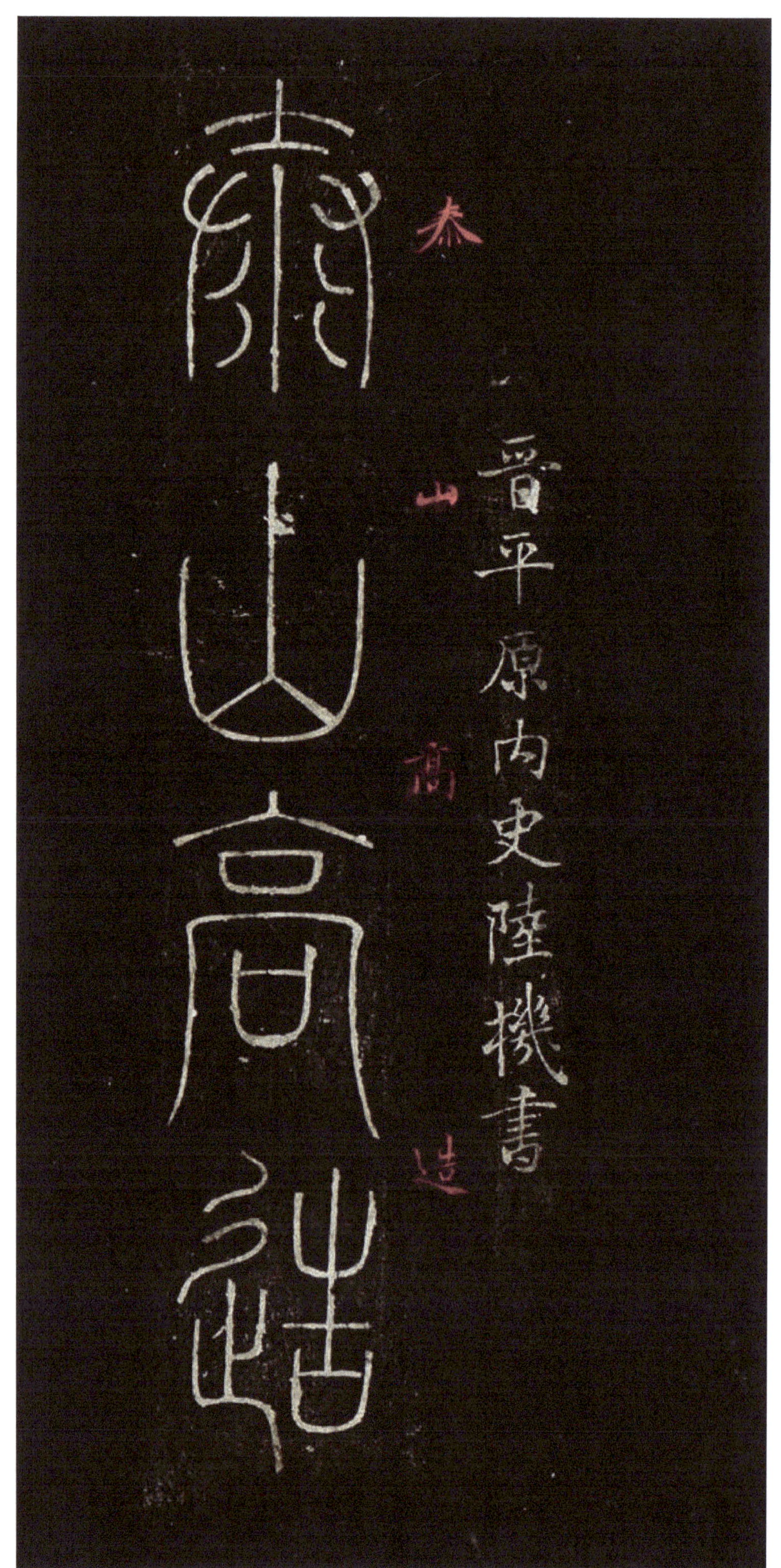

晉平原內史陸機書
泰山
高
造

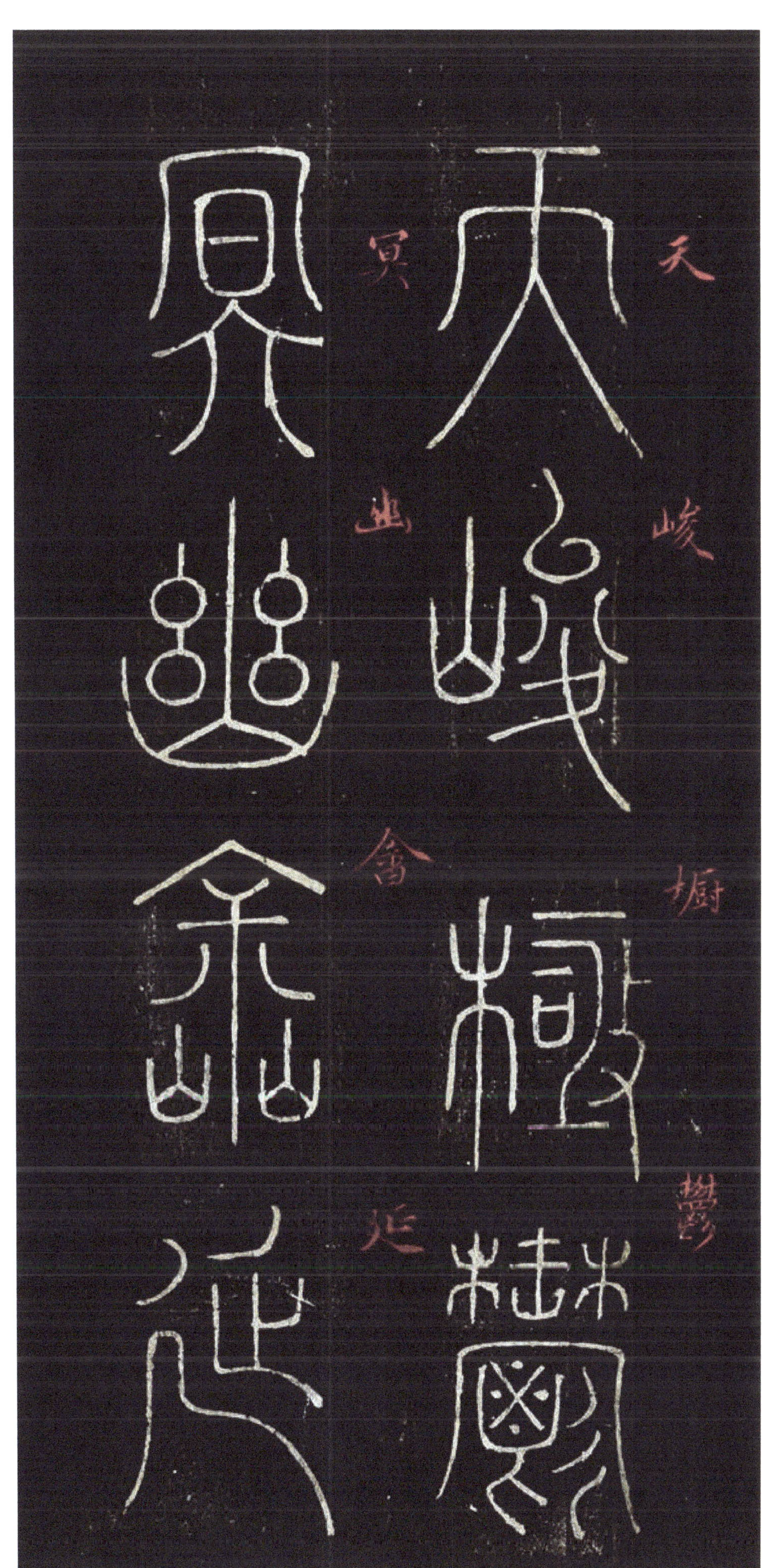

天
峻
厨
鬱
冥
迤
舍
延

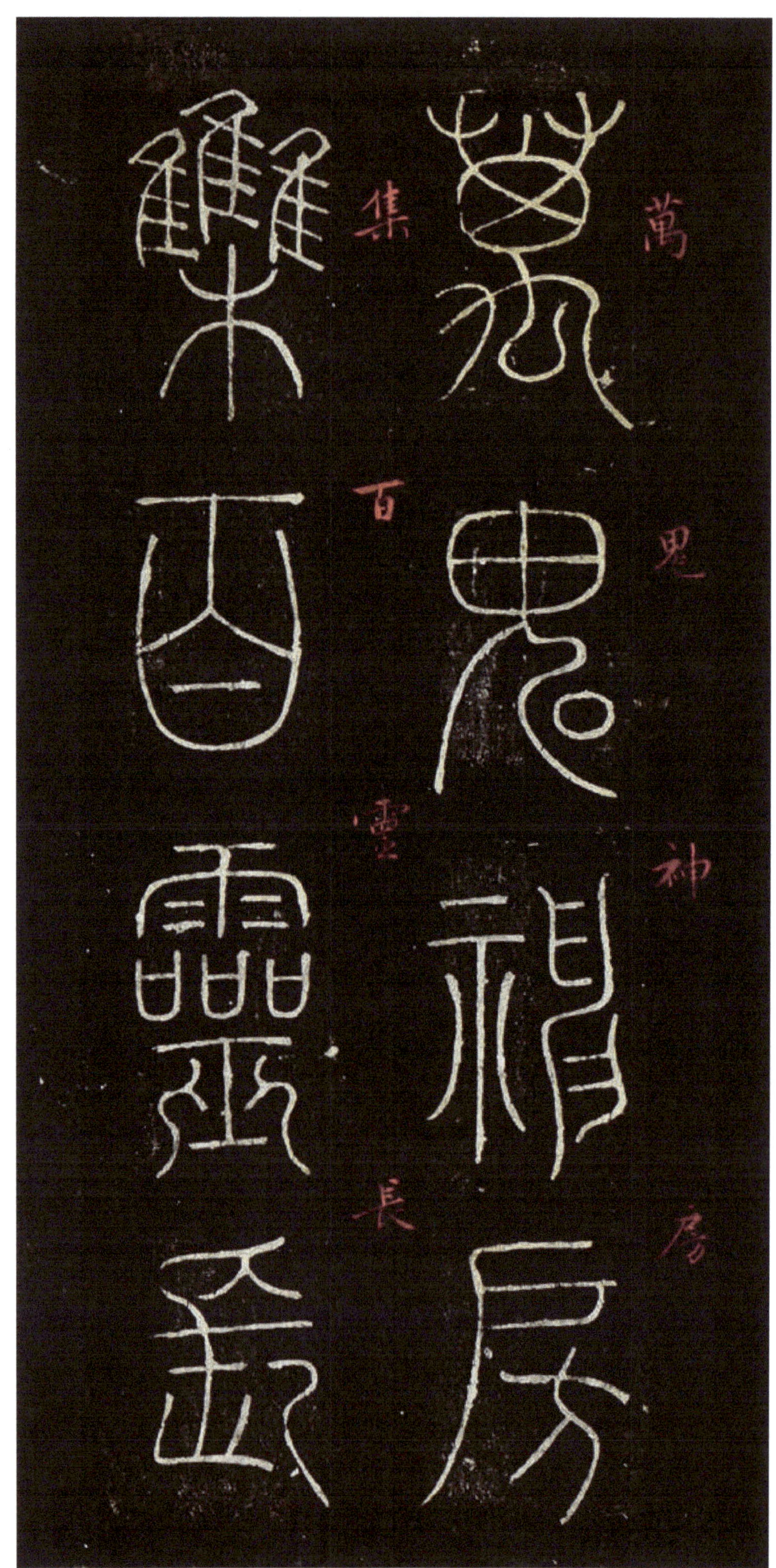

萬
集
里
百
神
靈
長
房

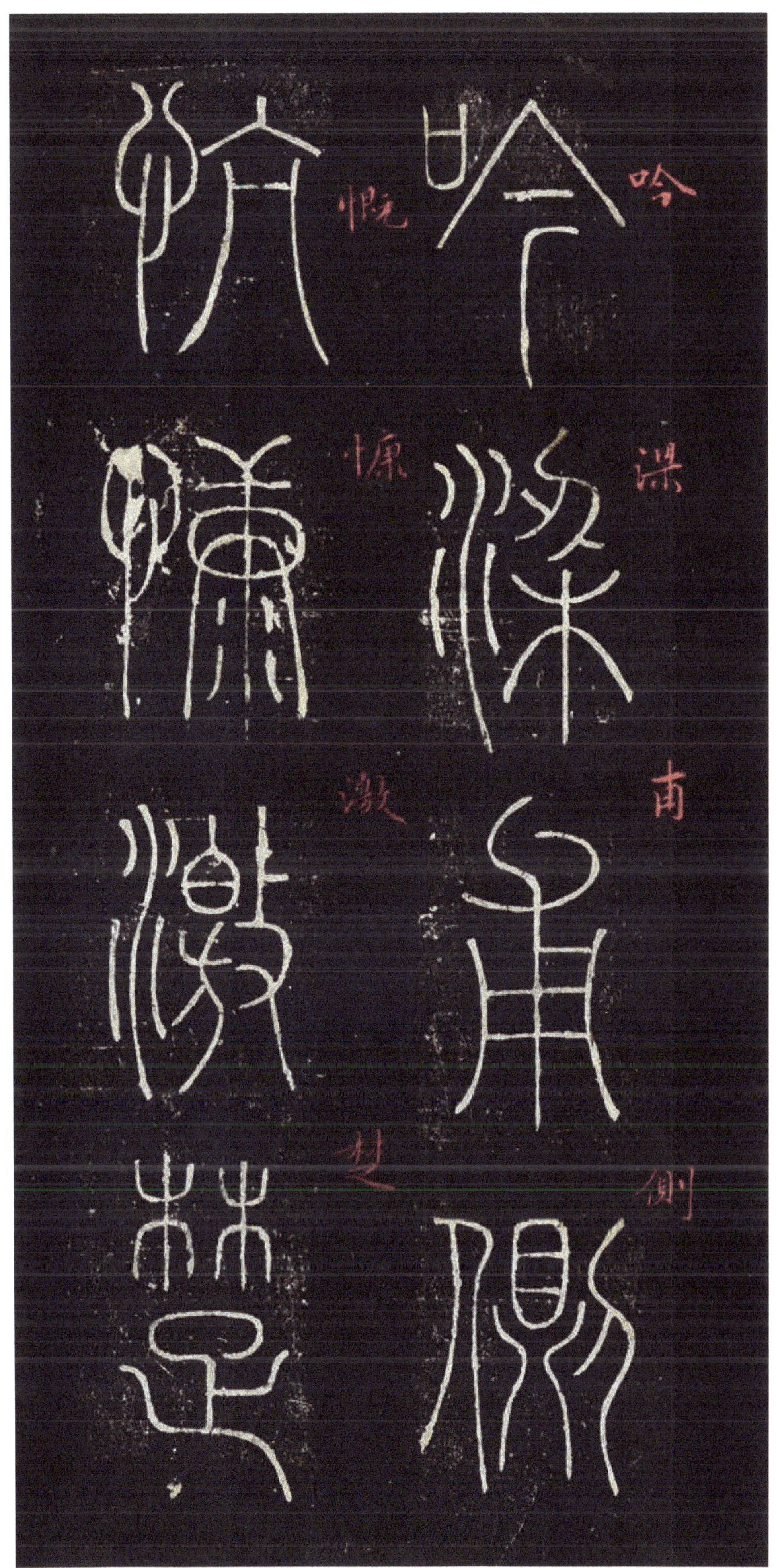

9

聲
聲
晉司徒王珉書
白

何如僕故乜敝力書不次王珉

敬首頓首上六囚如僕上六大

善蒙圓

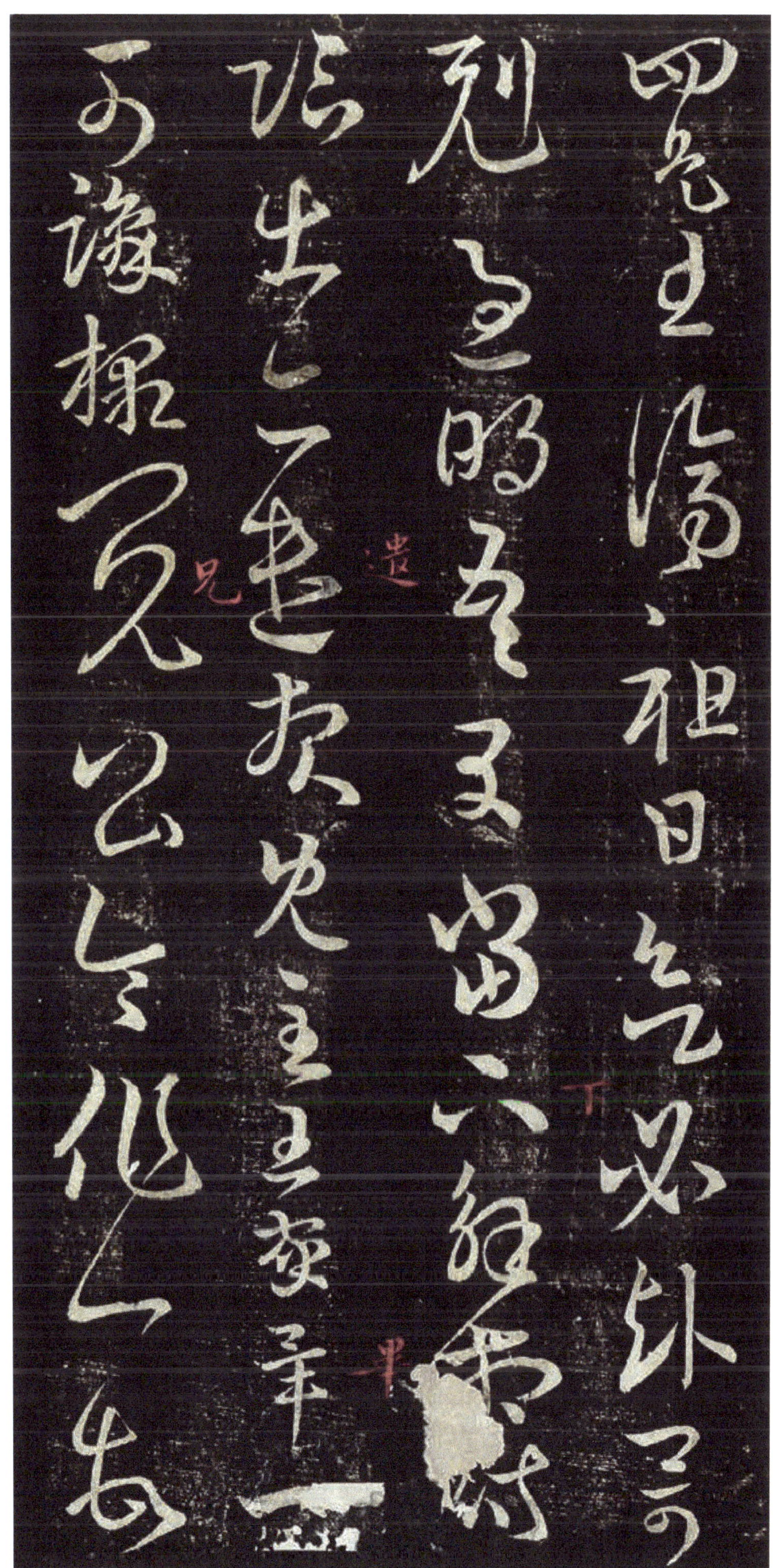

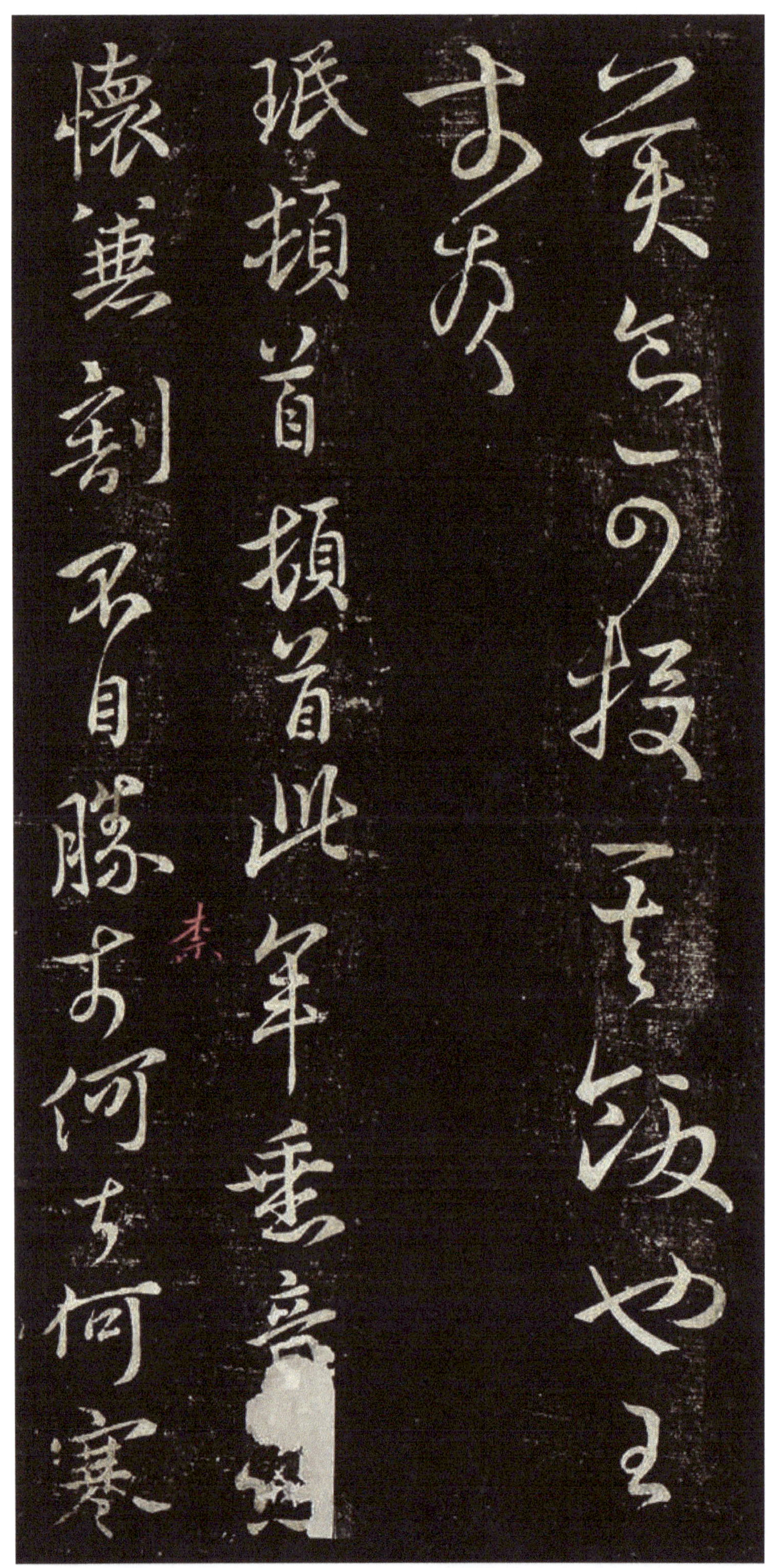
夫己之投重級也王
氏頓首頓首此年垂言
懷無割不自膝求何方何寒

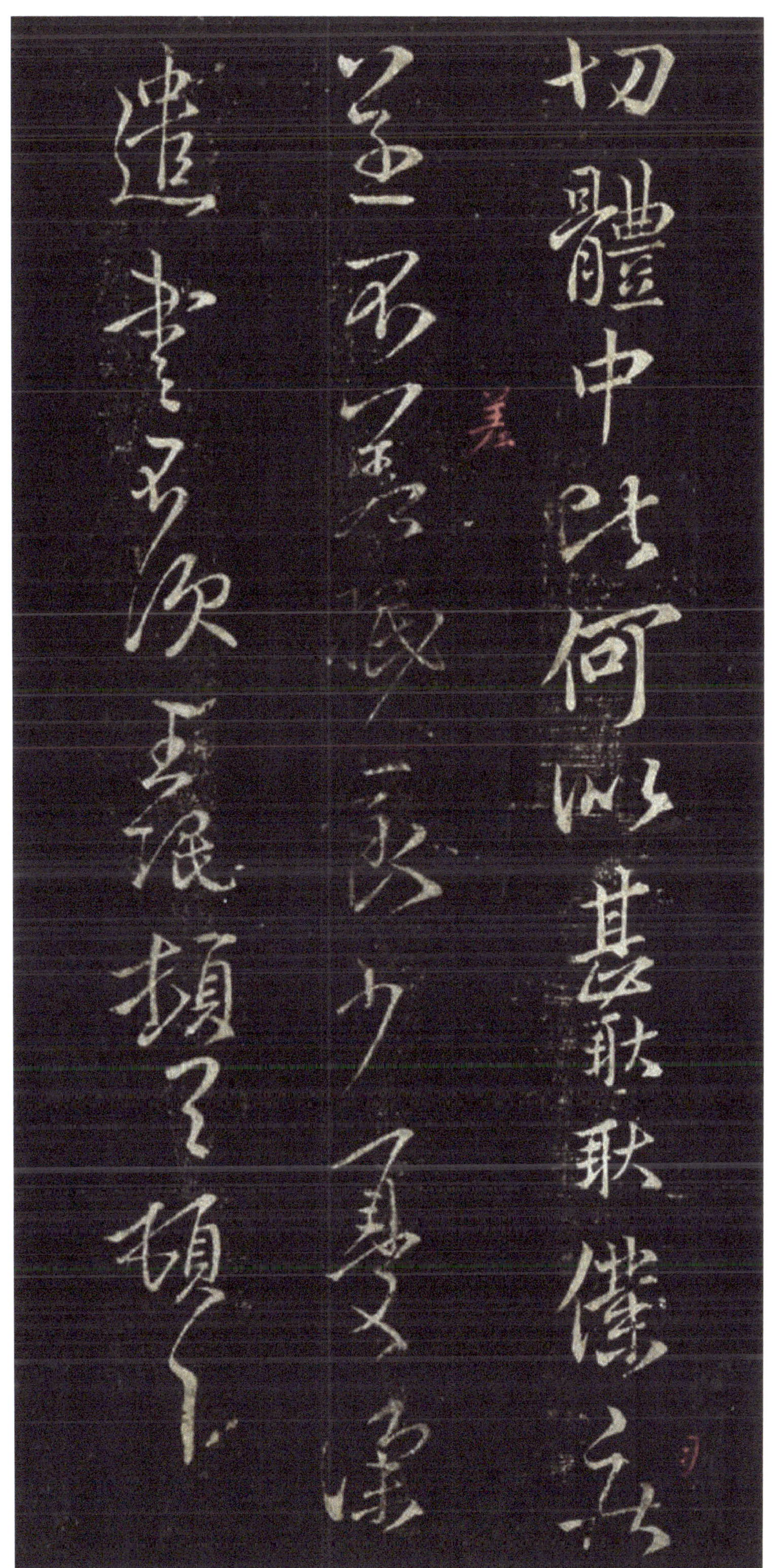

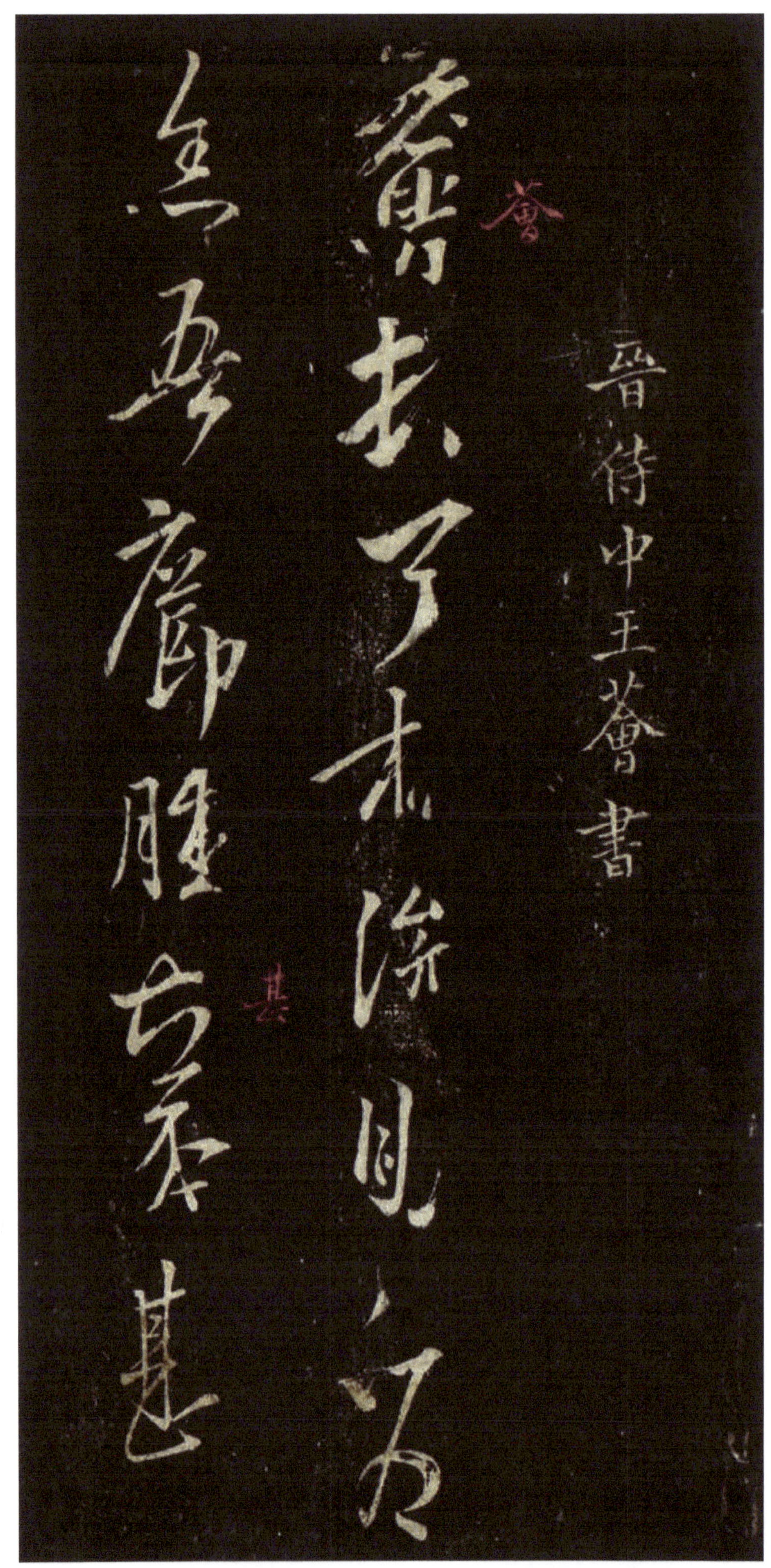
晉侍中王薈書

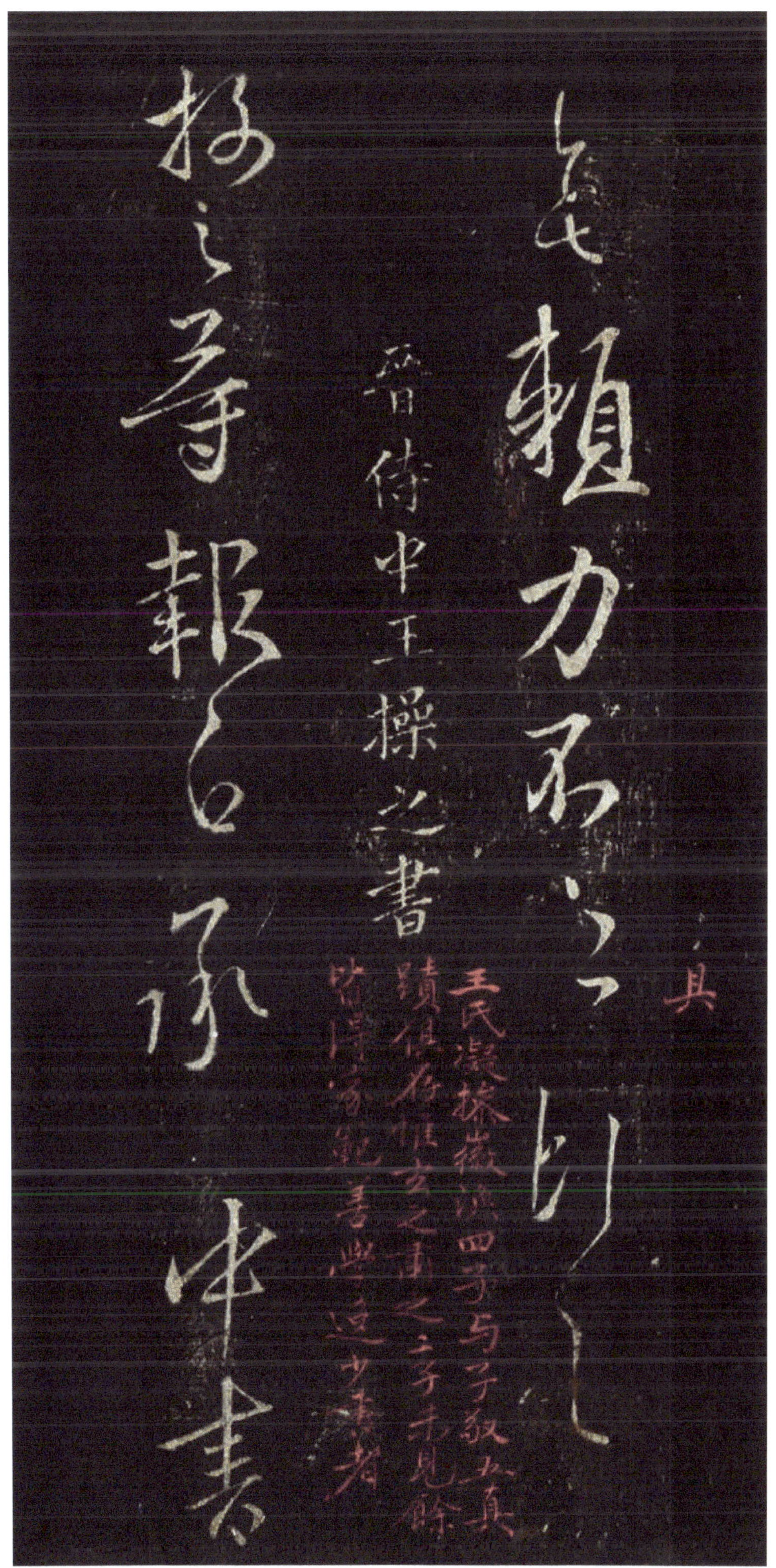

晉侍中王操之書

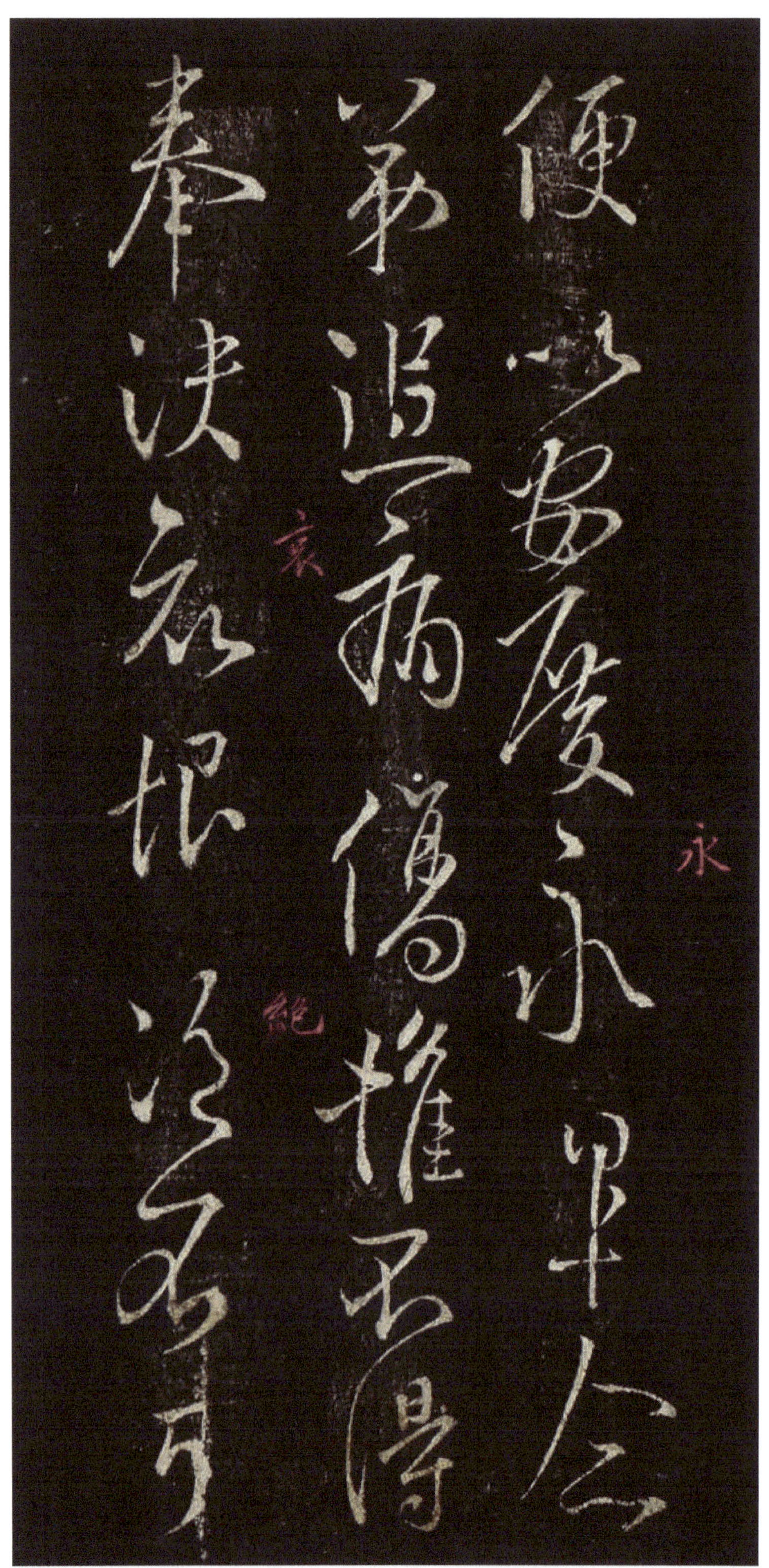
便安慶永小
承温傷摧哀
奉決恨得絶

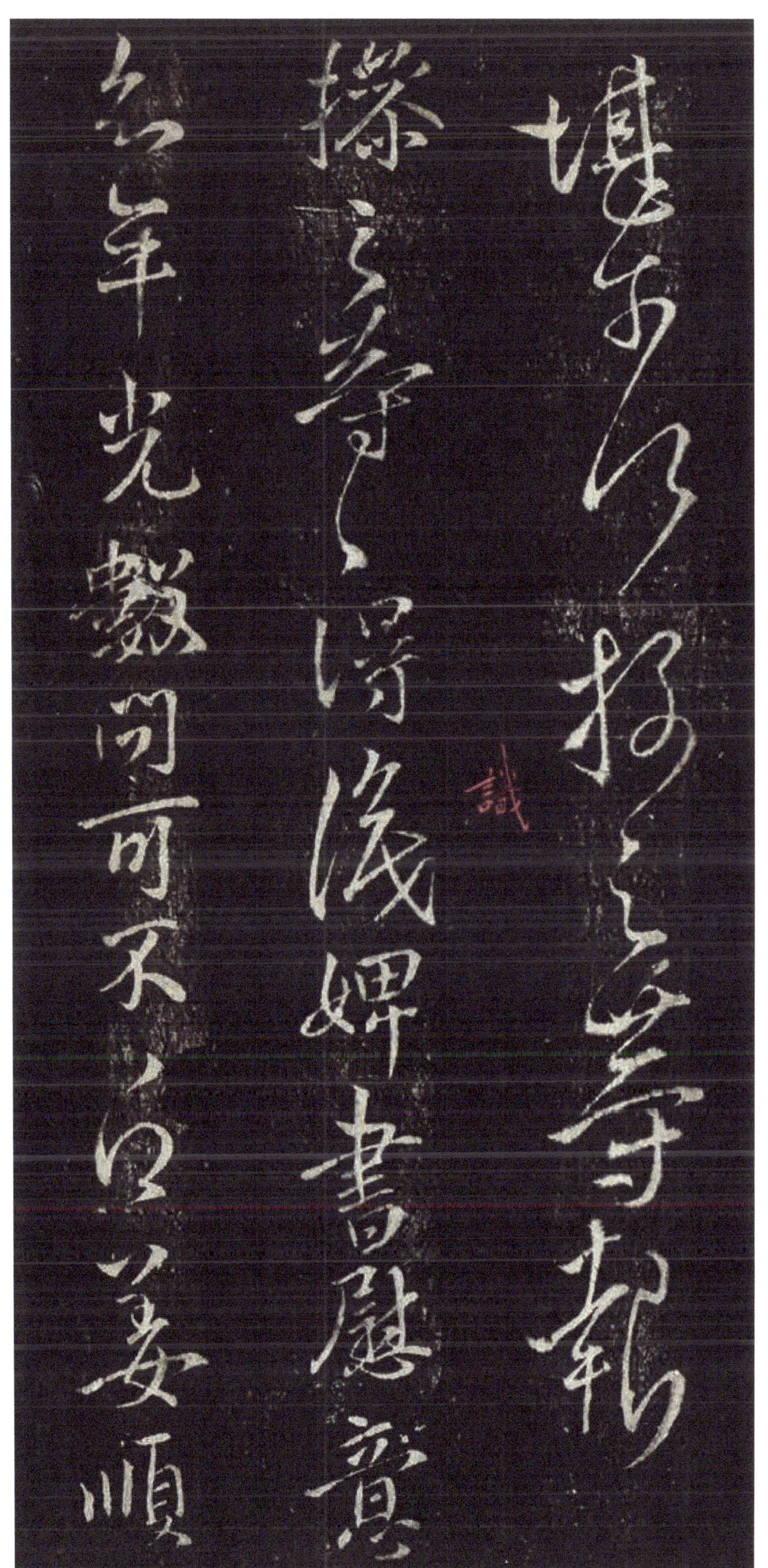

消息愁心擦旬

晉司徒王廙書

告諒靜媛靜儀靜姊此晦使

當假葵永痛抽剌忍情六割宋

自滕念㳙等追痛摧慟絕綿斷

絞何可堪任痛當奈何奈何省

奈何遣慮㘽涕不次廞頓

晉黃門郎王渙之書

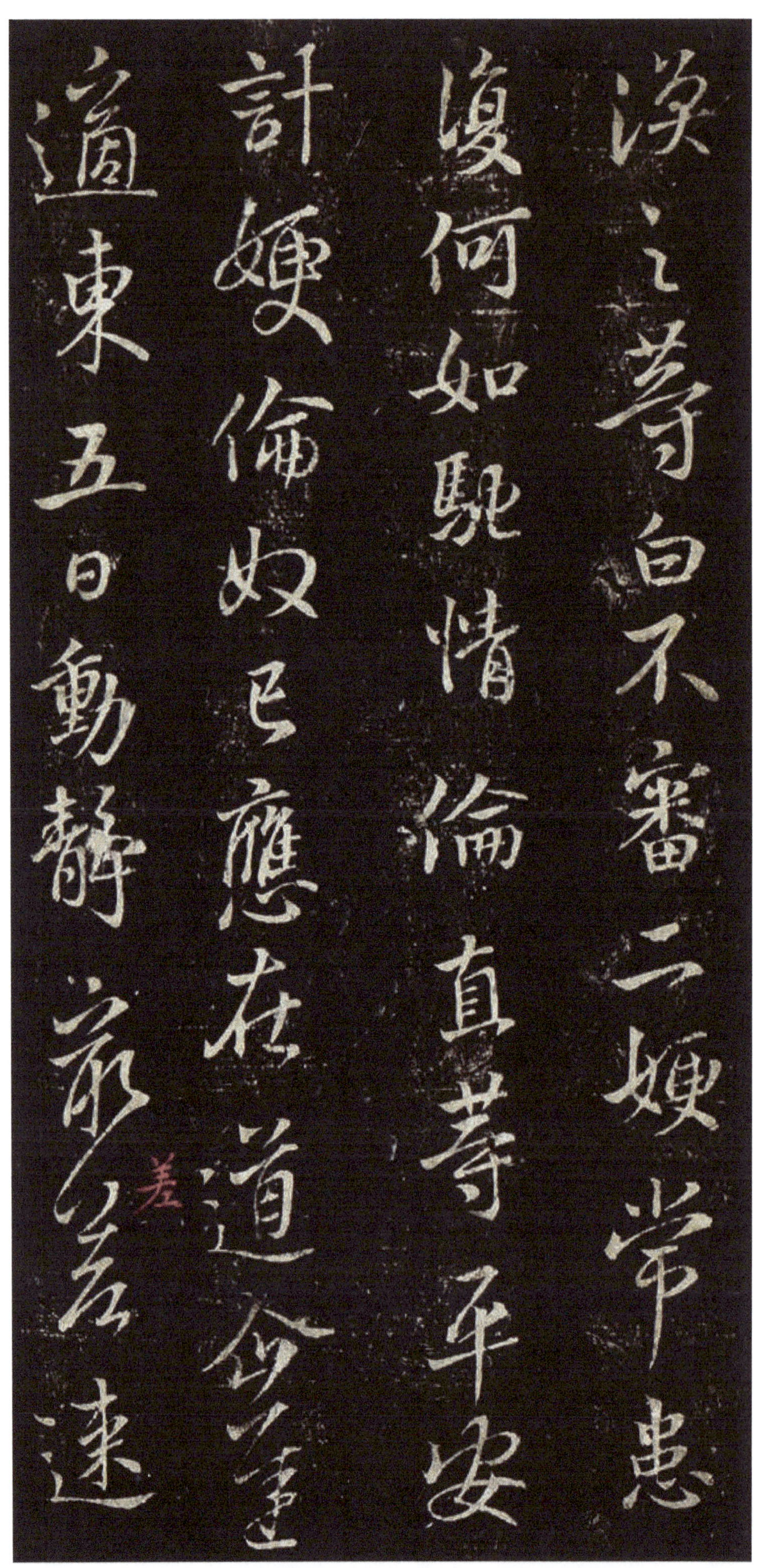
淡之等白不審二嫂常患
復何如馳情倫直尋平安
計婢倫奴已應在道逢
遠道東五日動靜郷差速

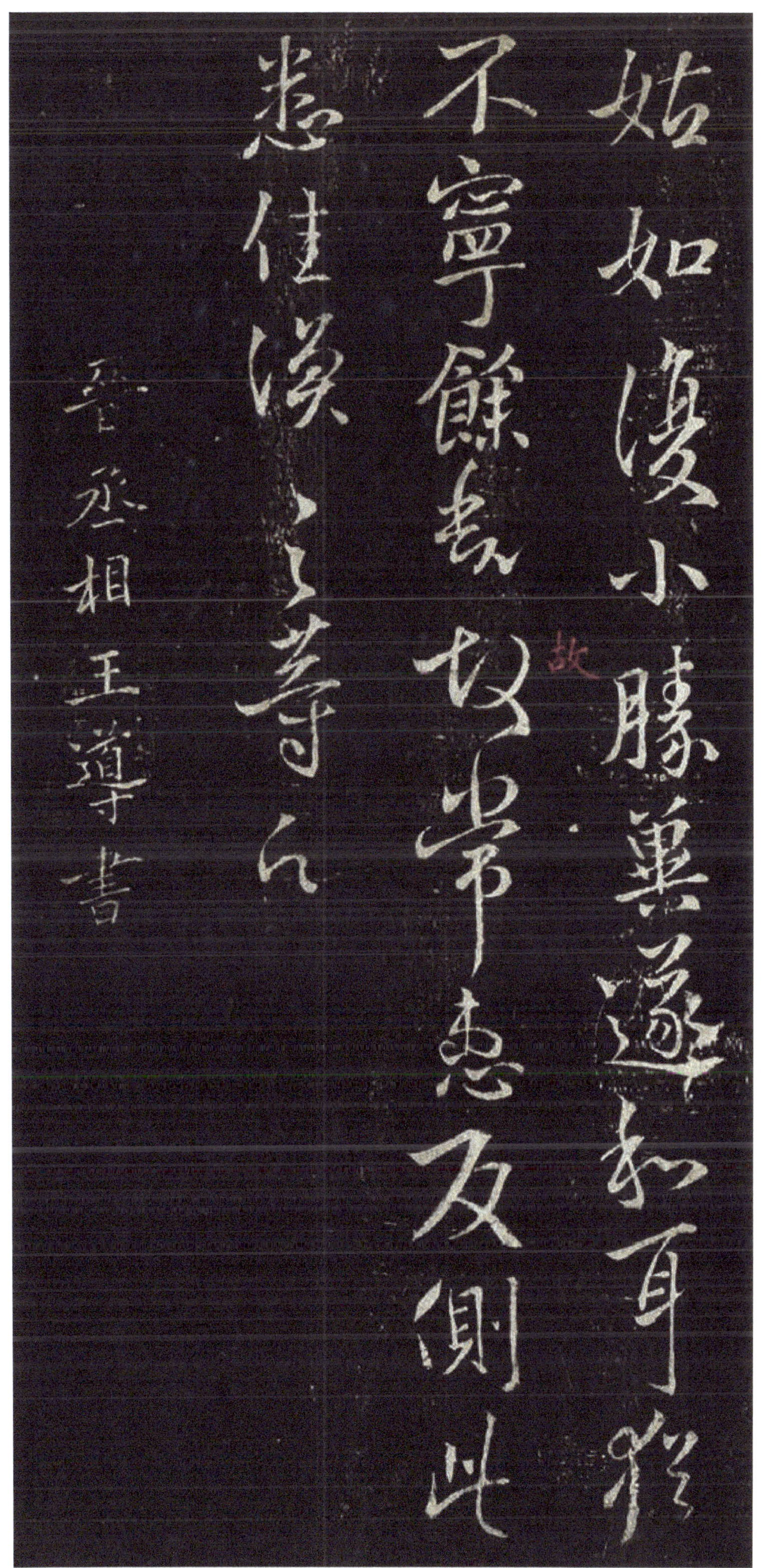
姑如復小腆裏遐知有耳
不寧餘惠如常惠及側此
悲佳深之等也
晉丞相王導書

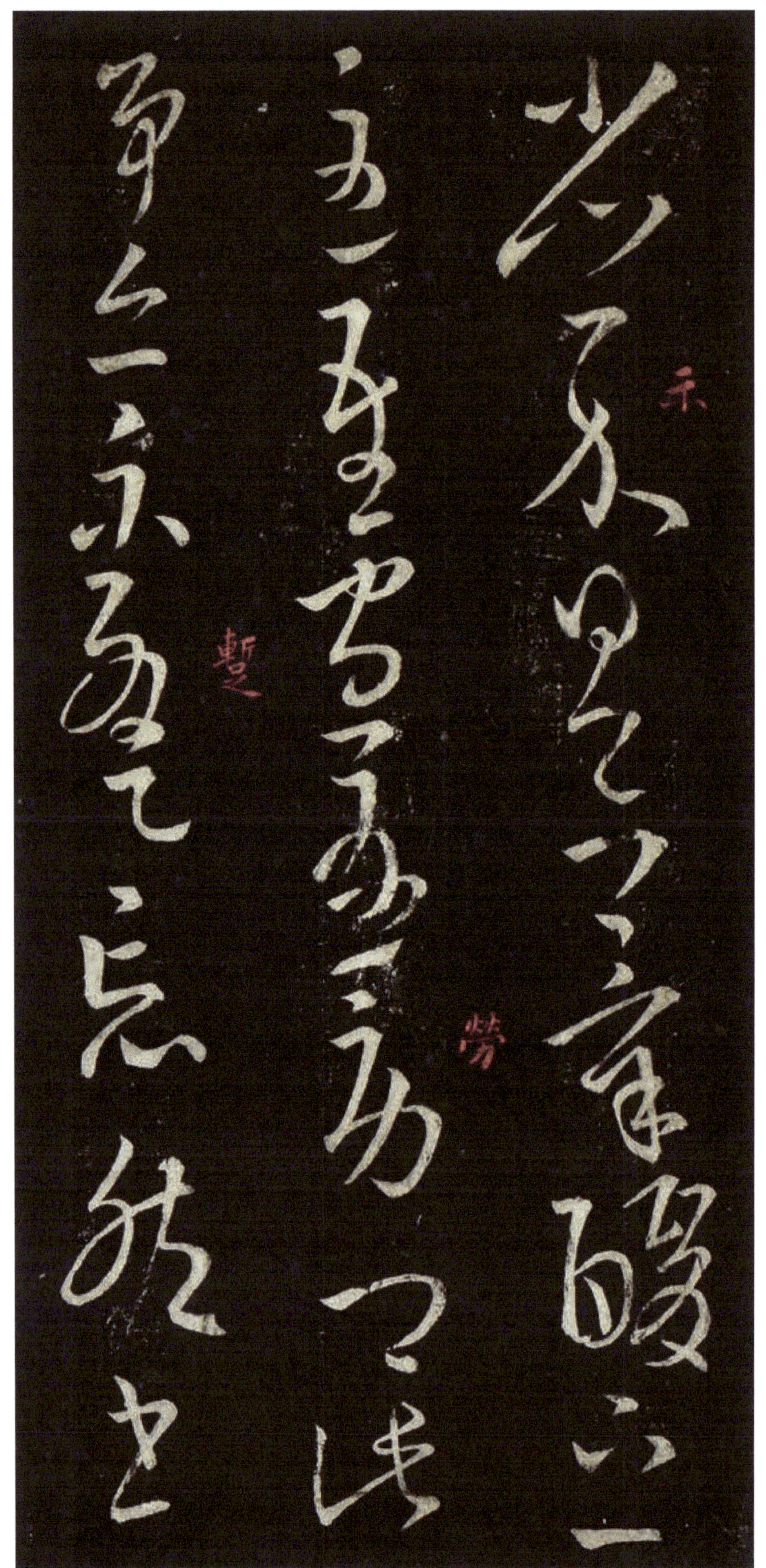
禾
暫
勞

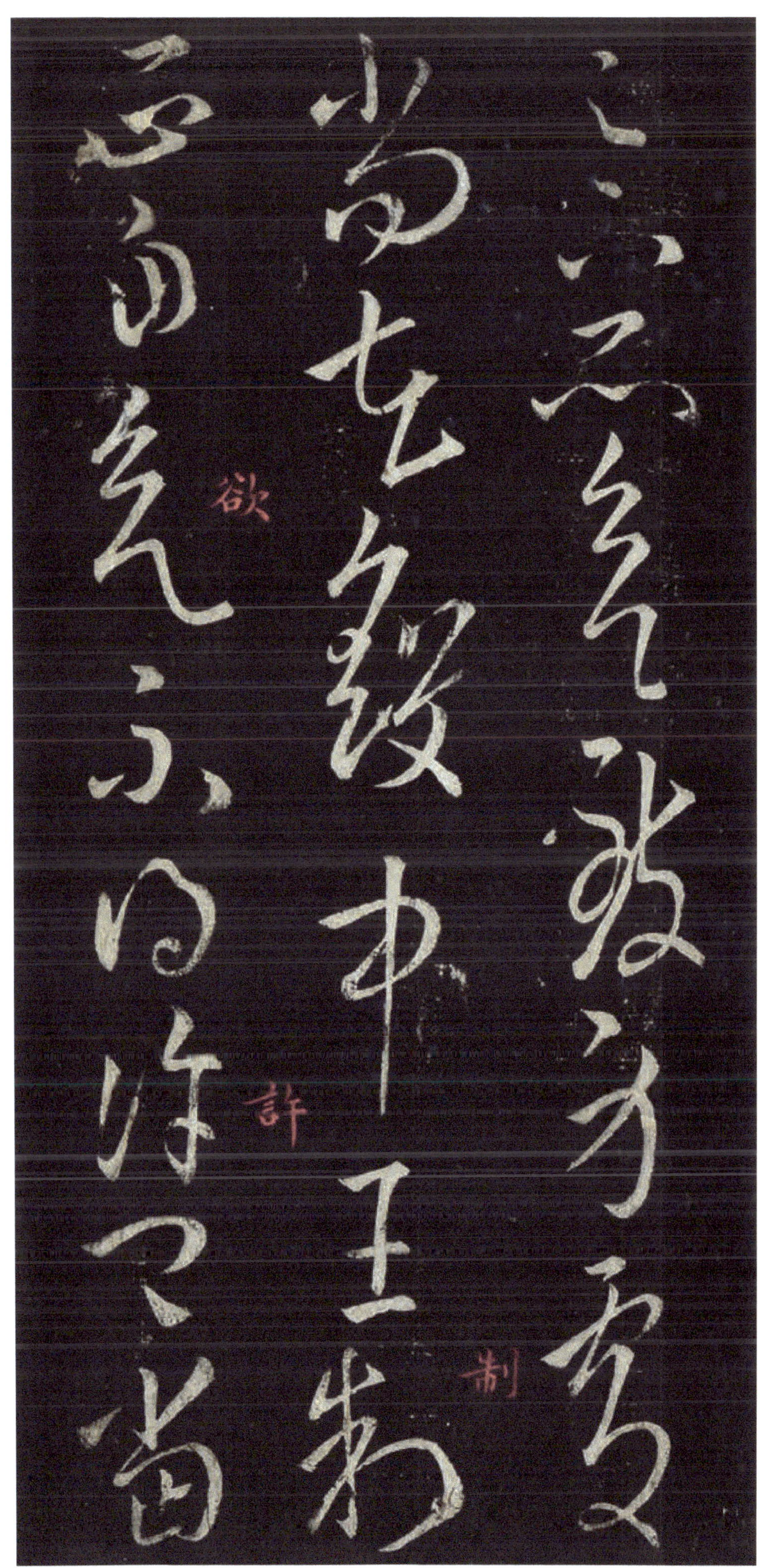
欲
許
制

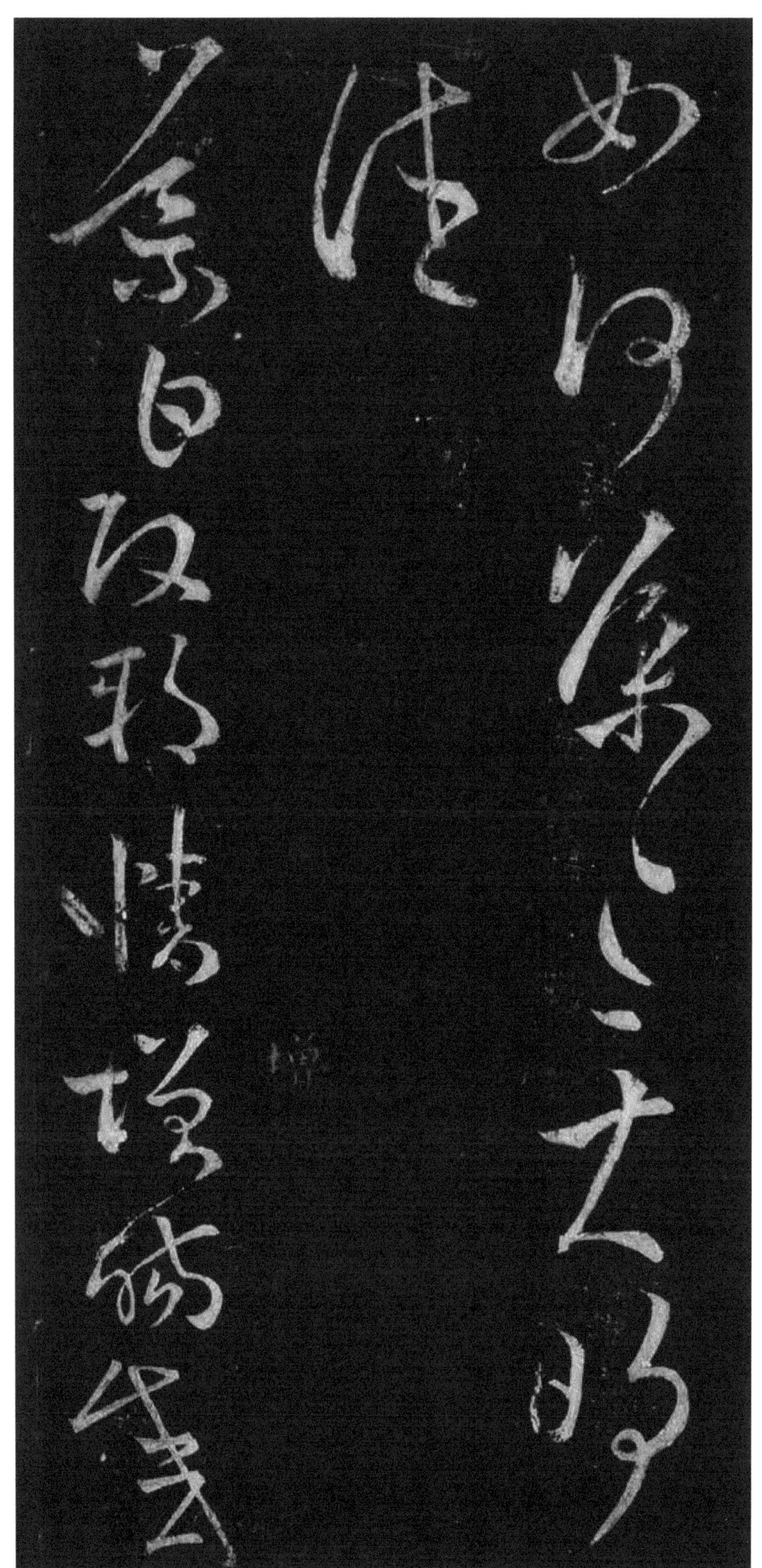

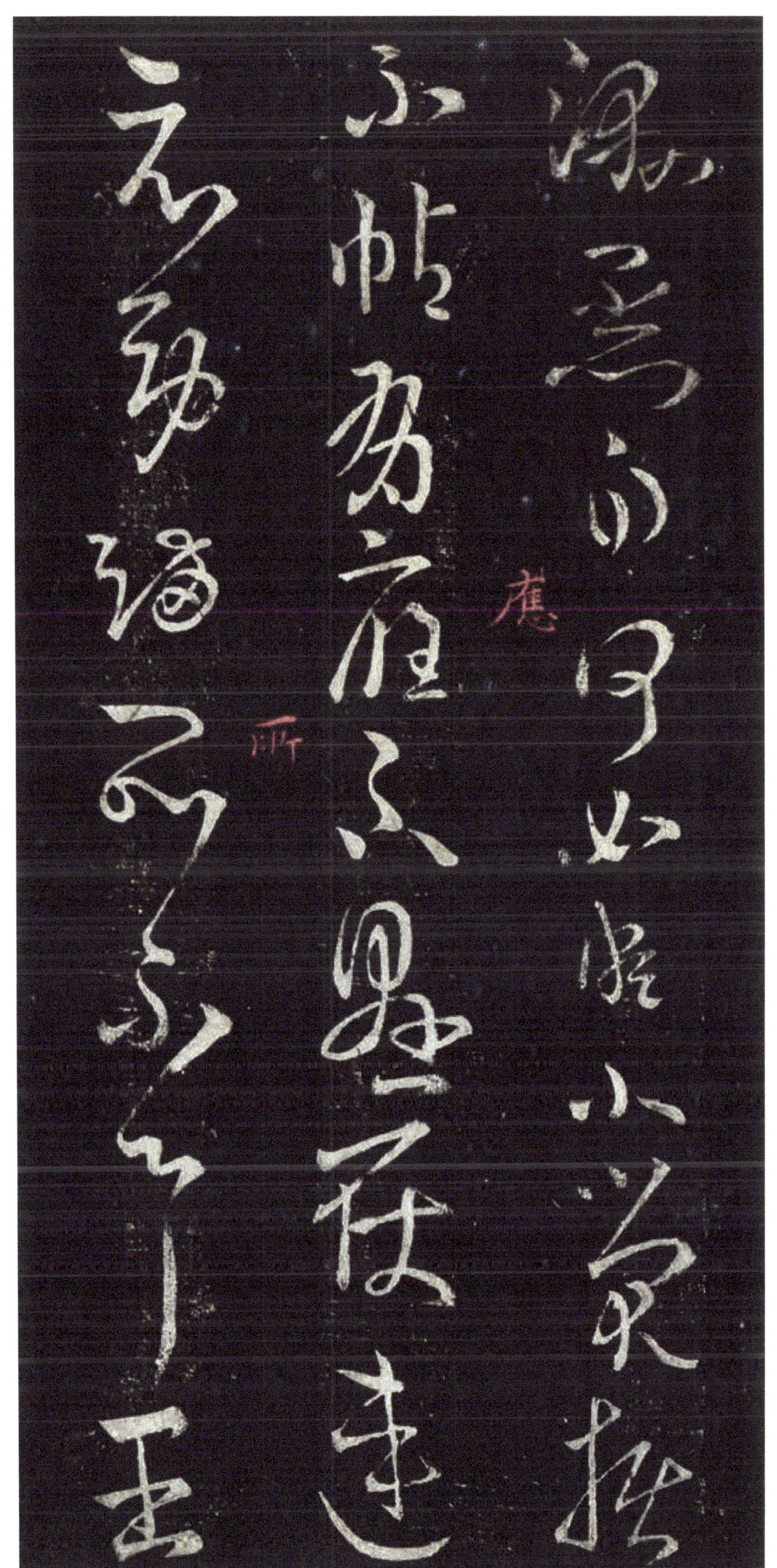

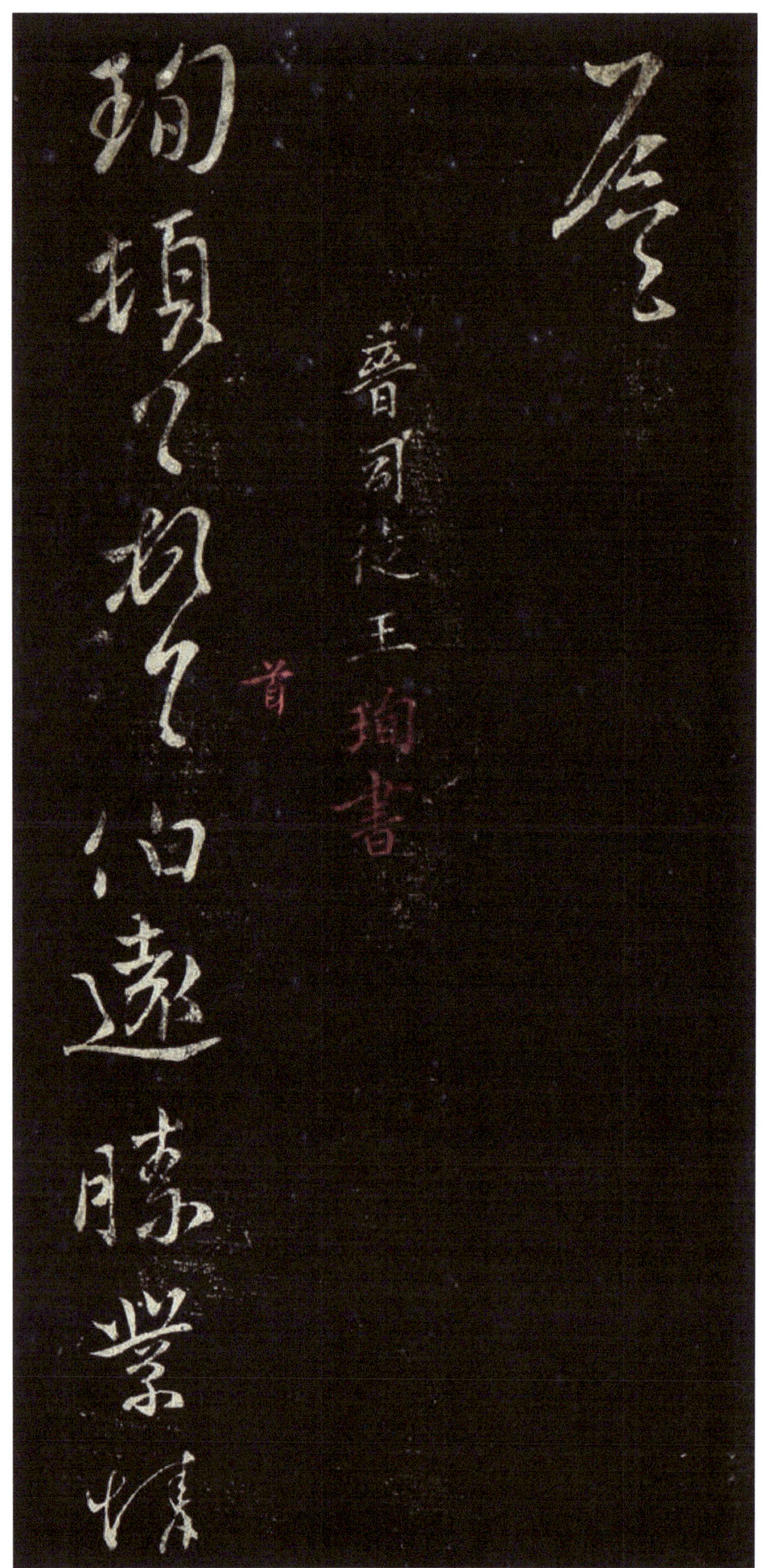

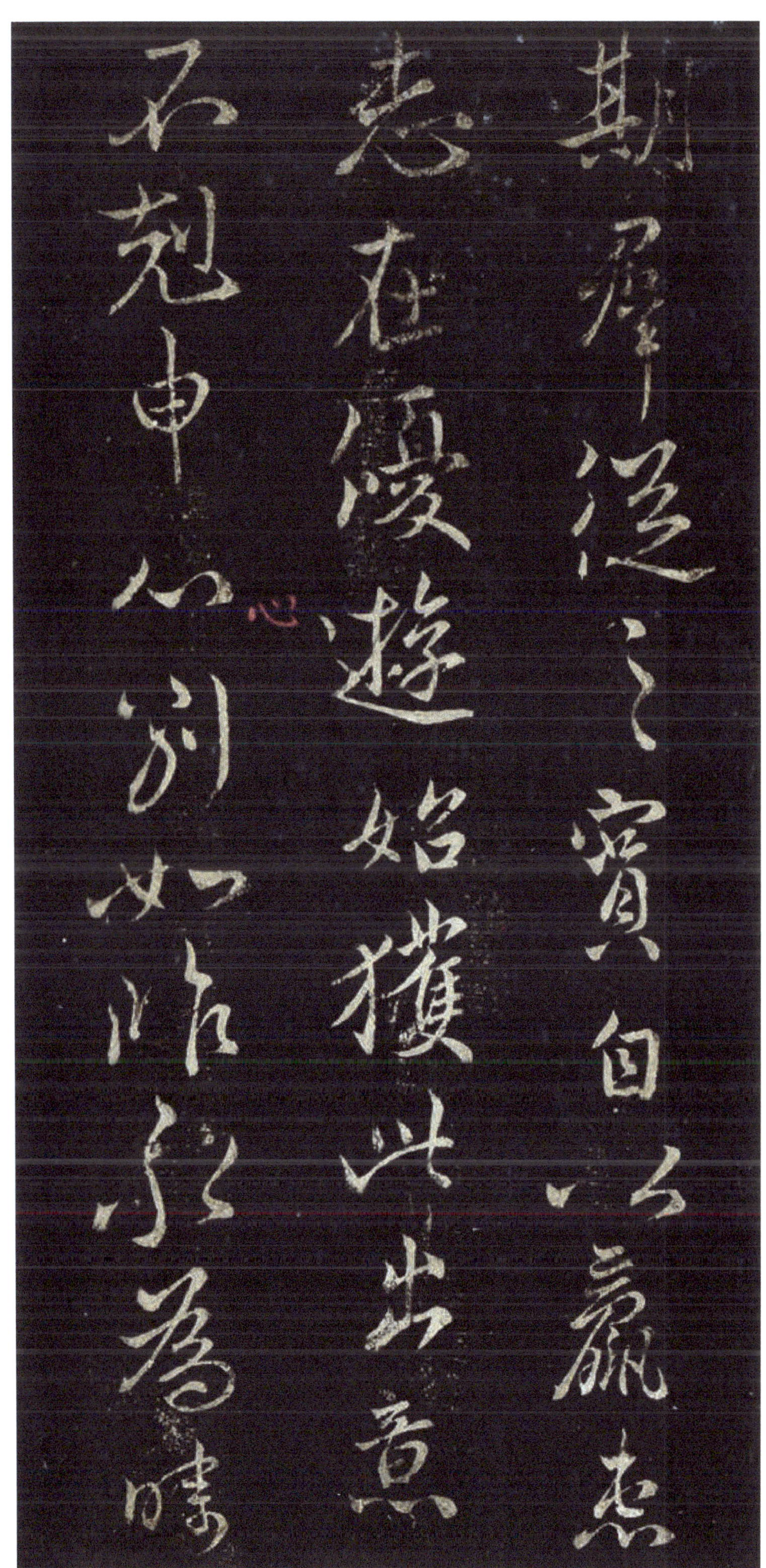

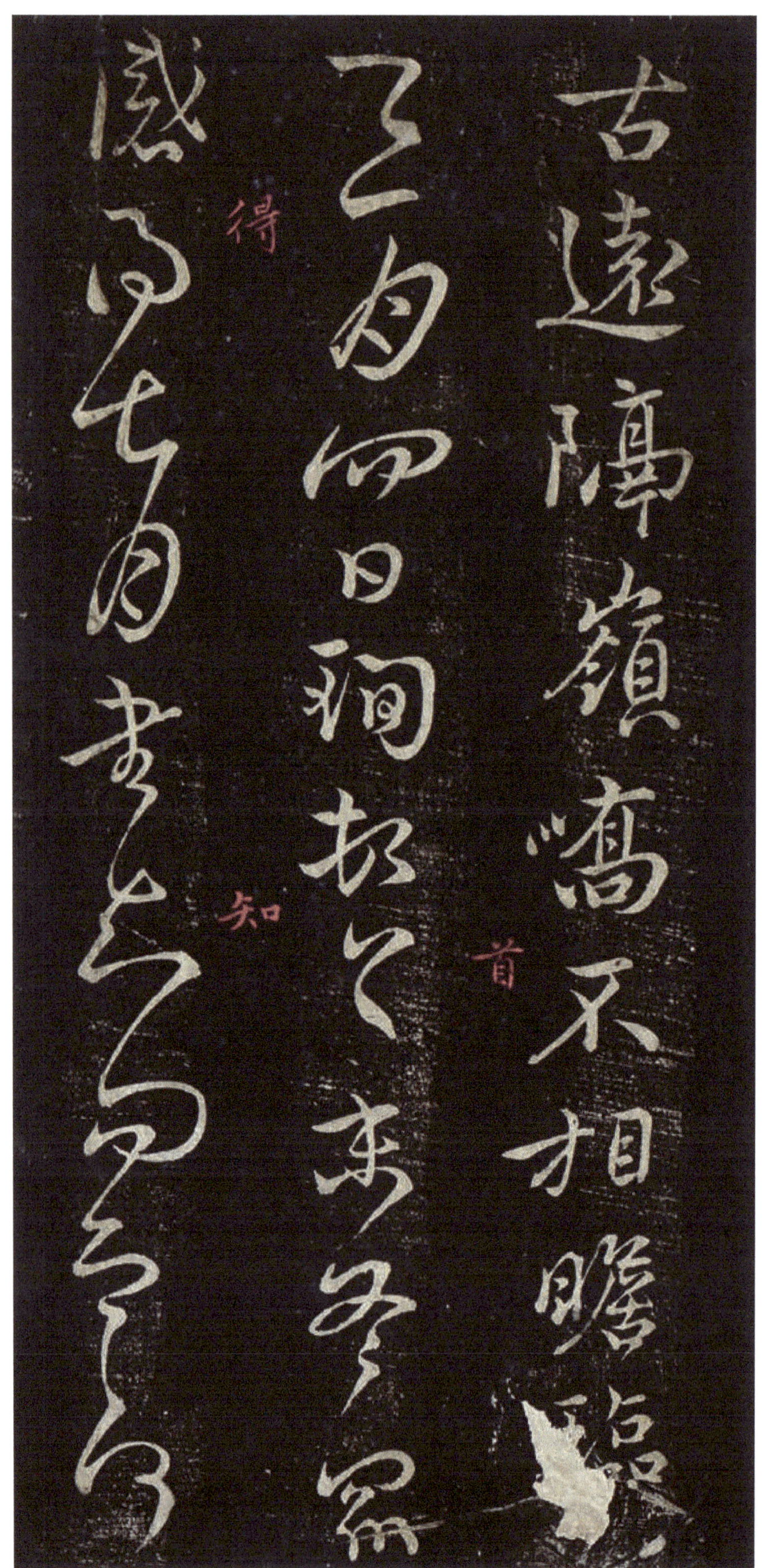
若遠隔嶺嶠不相瞻臨
又為四日洞始不知
感

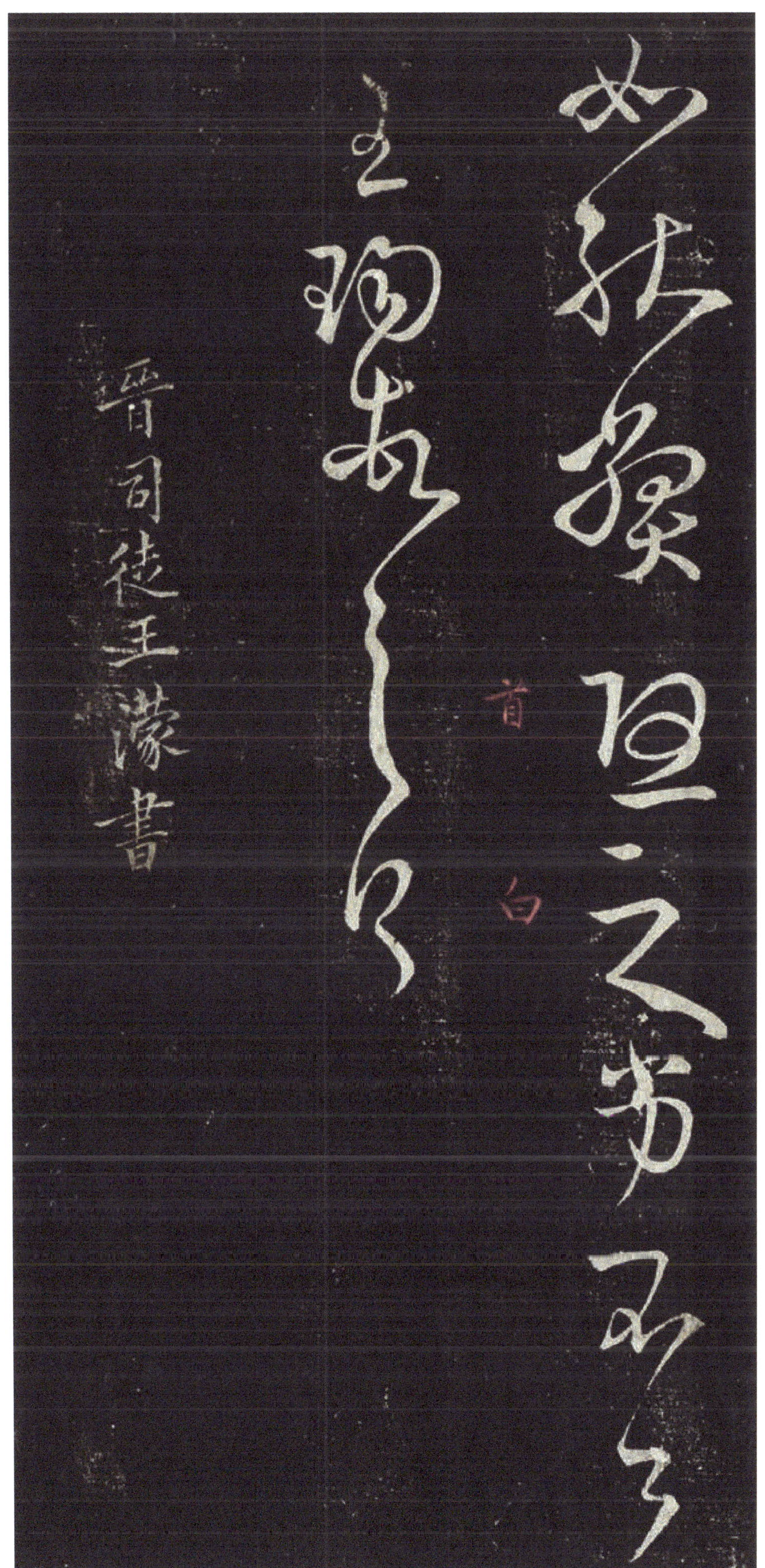

濠死罪前以比得諸葛餘抗書

及此義故誠宜敦率然其名此縣

近十年經歷四五長吏矣欲緝其

時吏則十無一在欲調民則不知時

何為辭且諸葛僕尉之弟如是

餘杭以情料之當非至困者顏

便以下官歲谷之謹白濠死罪

晉中書令王洽書

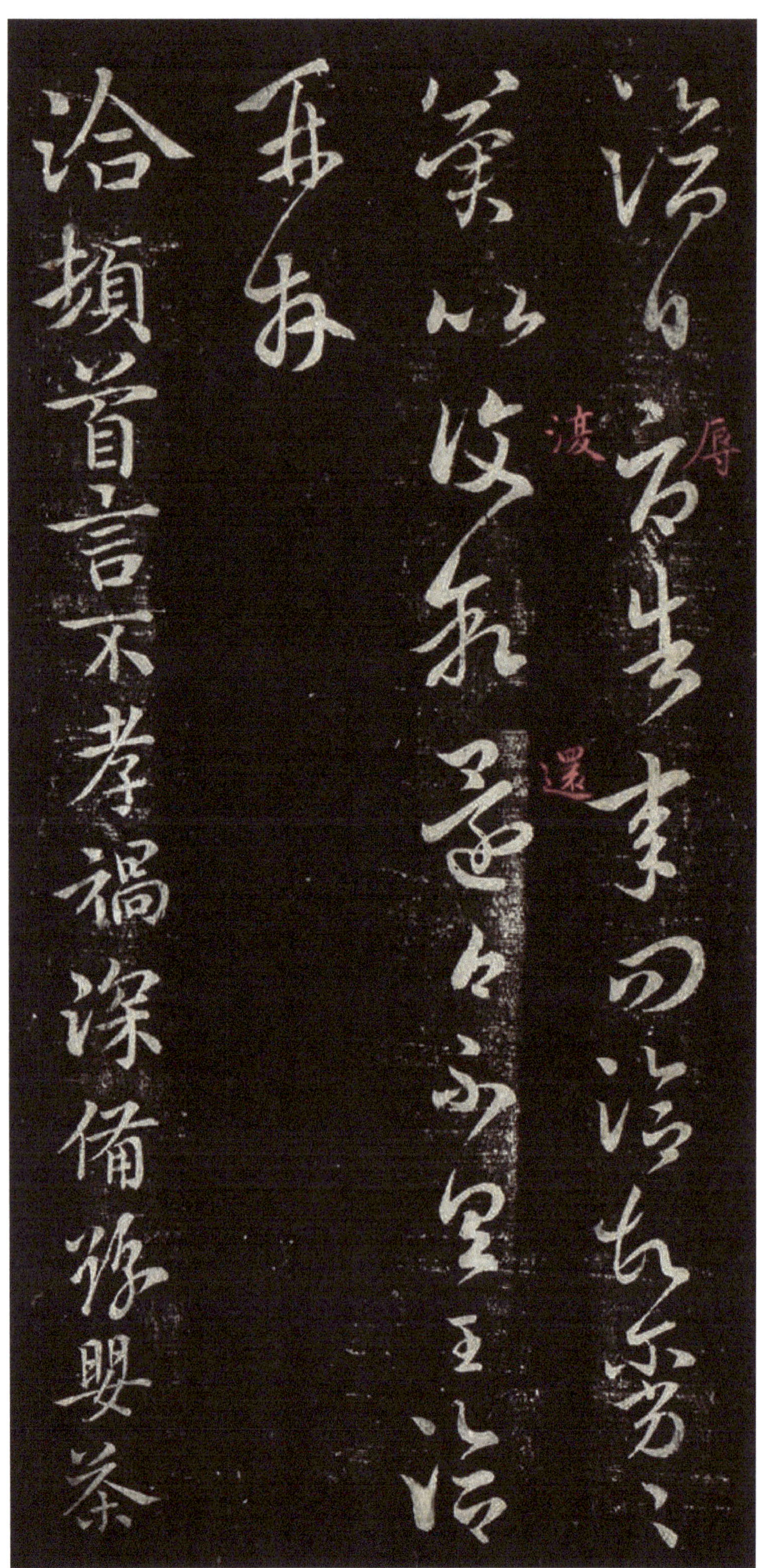

每陰恃己兄仁愛之訓冀終一百年
永有憑奉何圖慈兄一旦背棄乖
彌哀摧肝心如抽痛毒煩冤不
堪忍酷當奈何痛當　何重告慟

至感增斷絕執筆哽涕不知慶

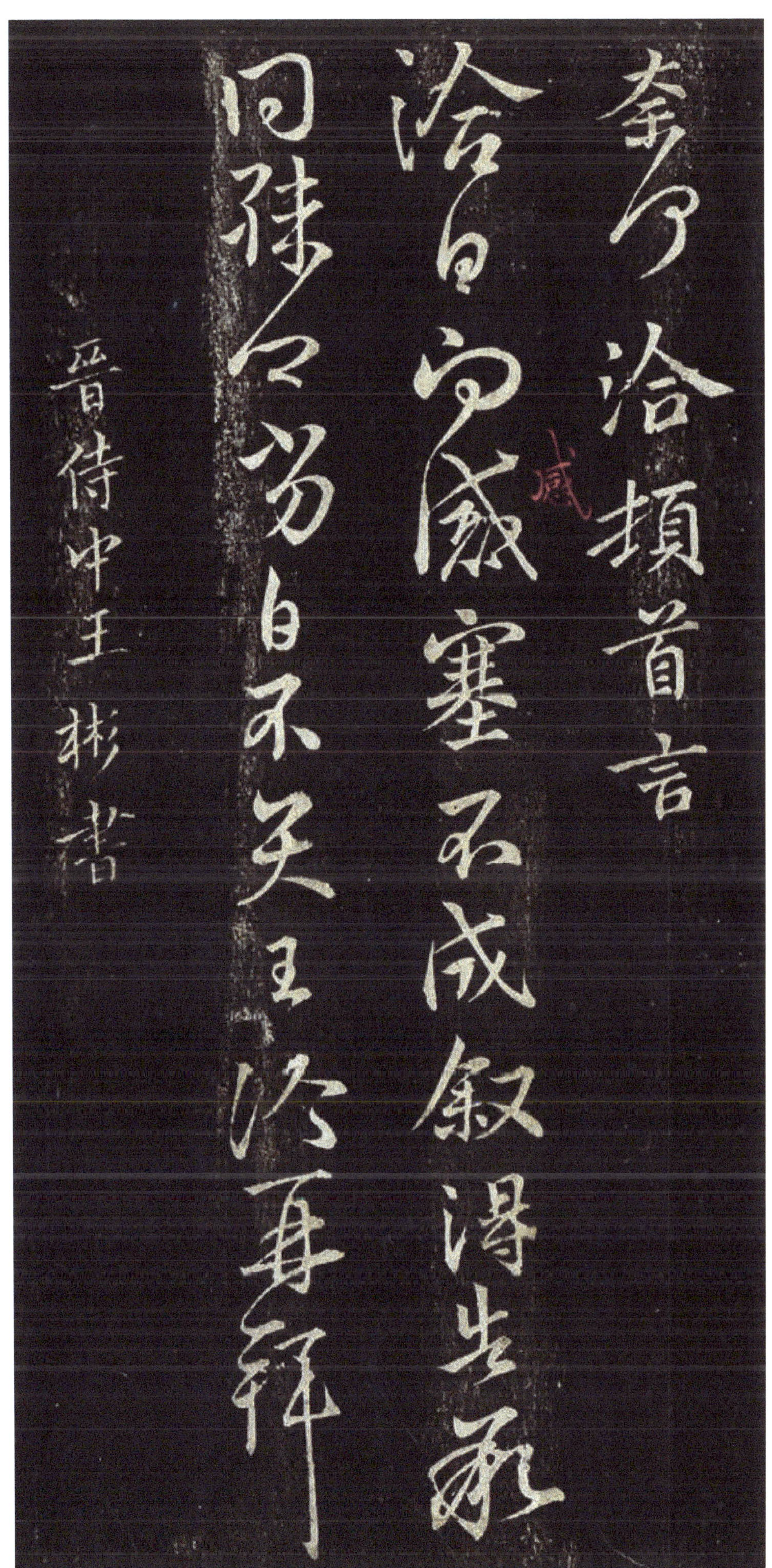

奈□洽頓首言
洽白威塞不成敘得出承
同陟力勿自不天旺涉更祥
晉侍中王彬書

晉黃門郎 王徽之書

二日告民女新月欲推不自勝

何念痛纂不可任口踈至蔬

故異憂懸心雨濕熱復多以食

不吾辱勞並頃勿没擊日還

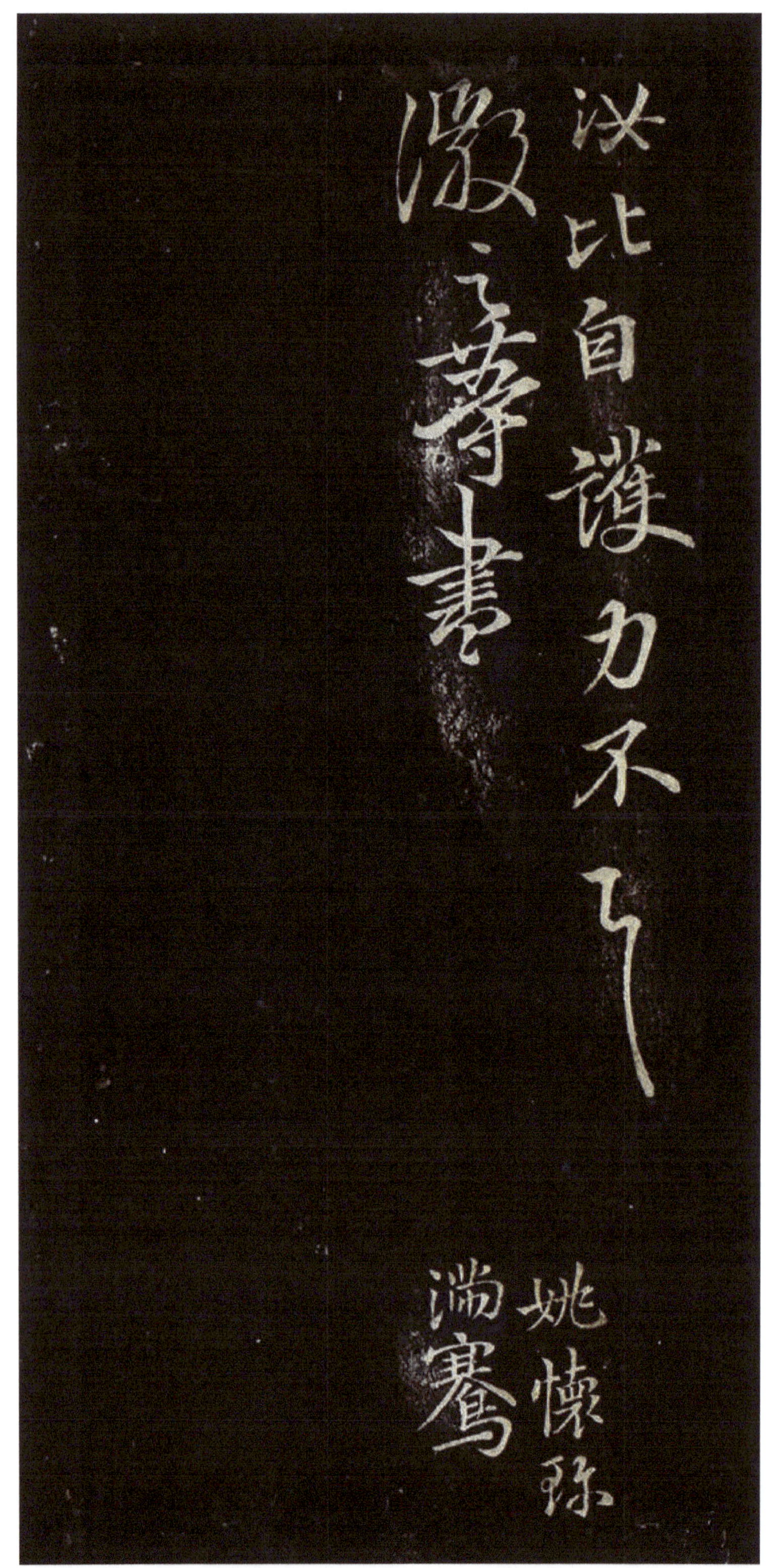

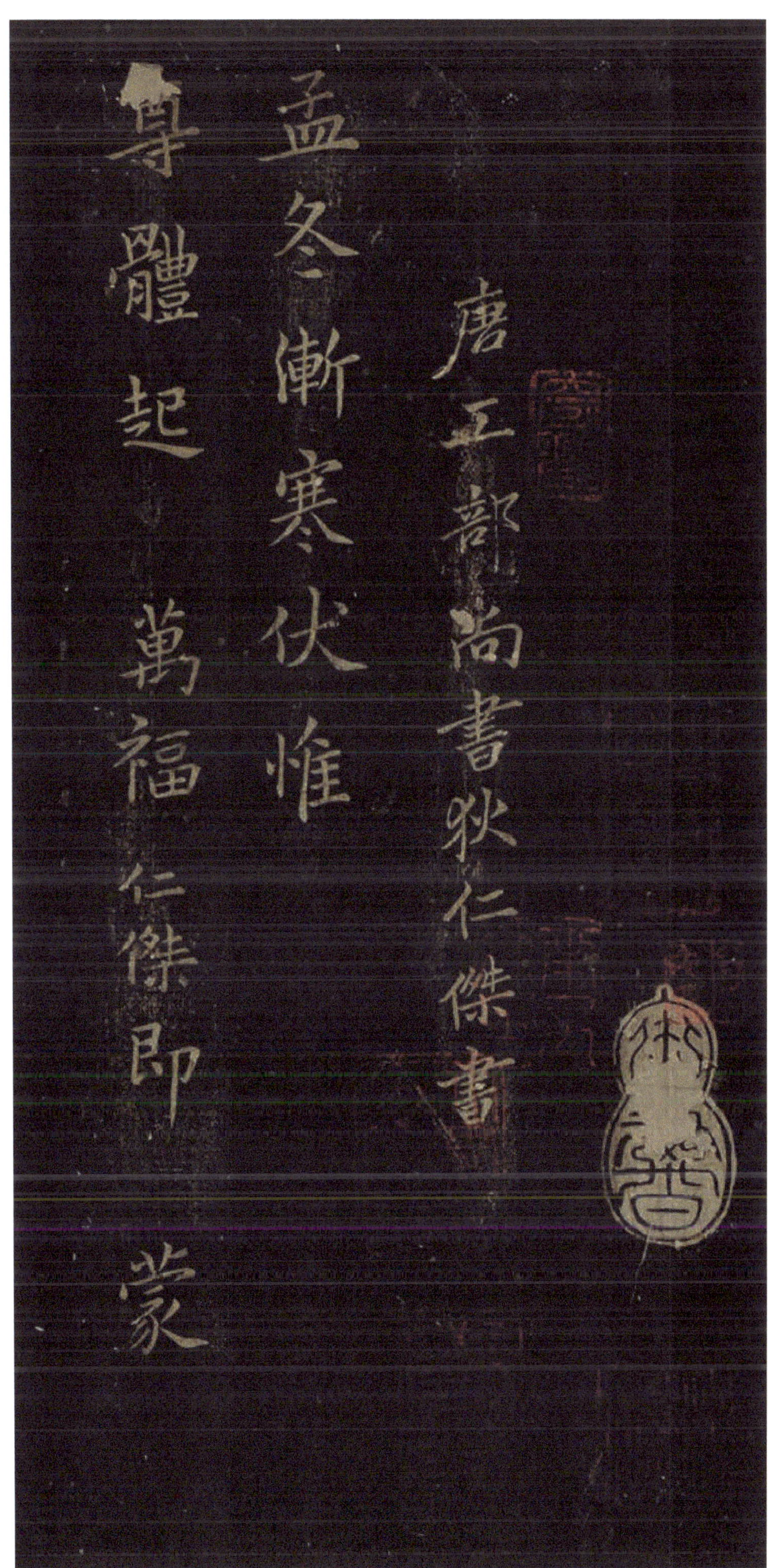

唐工部尚書狄仁傑書
孟冬漸寒伏惟
尊體起居萬福仁傑即蒙

息不審近日
寢膳何似自成遠間將及半年
每屬紛仍曾無一扎惶悚之外攀
戀實深人使遠来　戢翰猥至慰

捧欣佩交集下懷兼有　　露出於
記念未期高會念望增深使迴
奉狀　起居陳
謝不宣謹狀

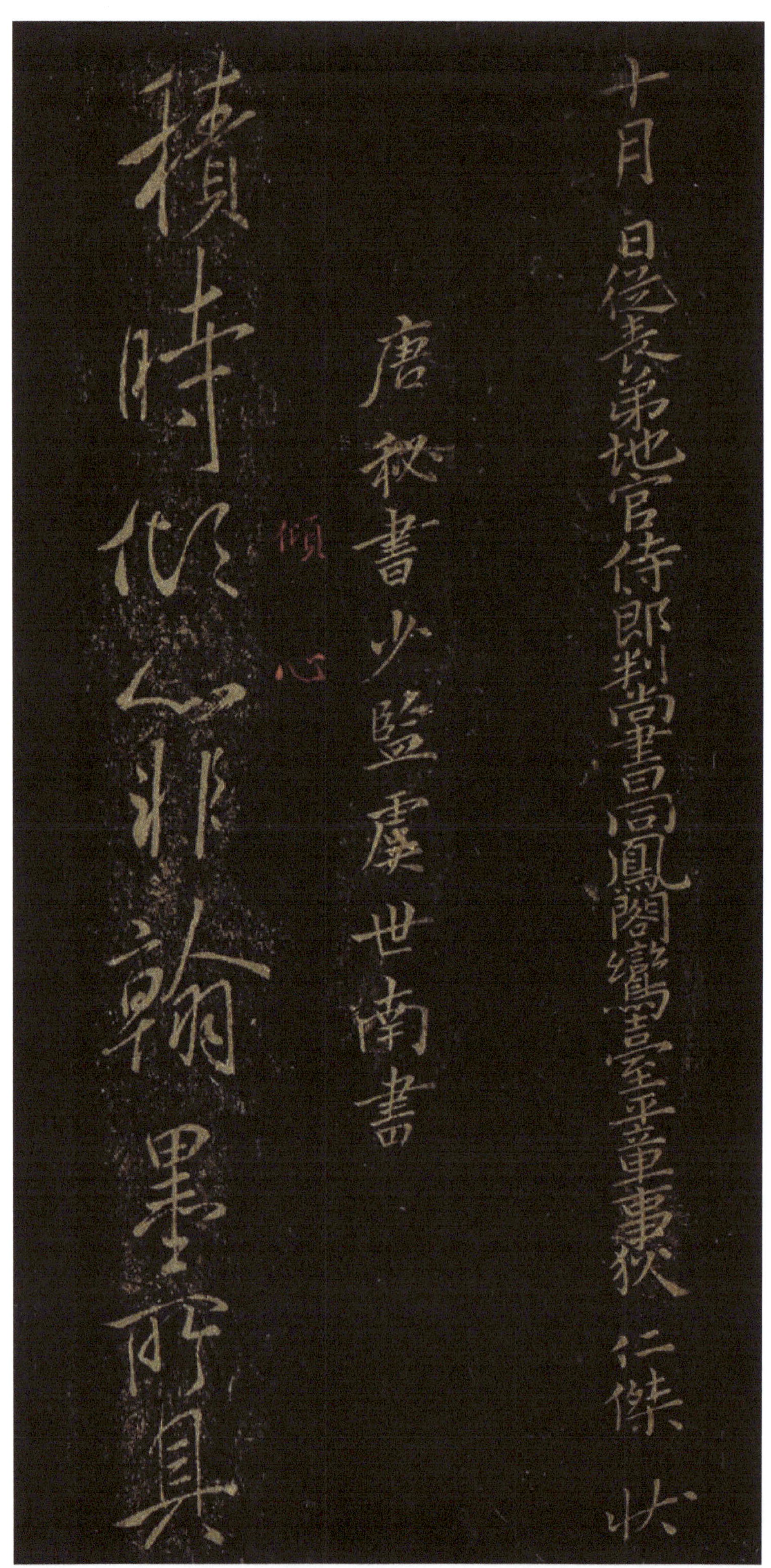

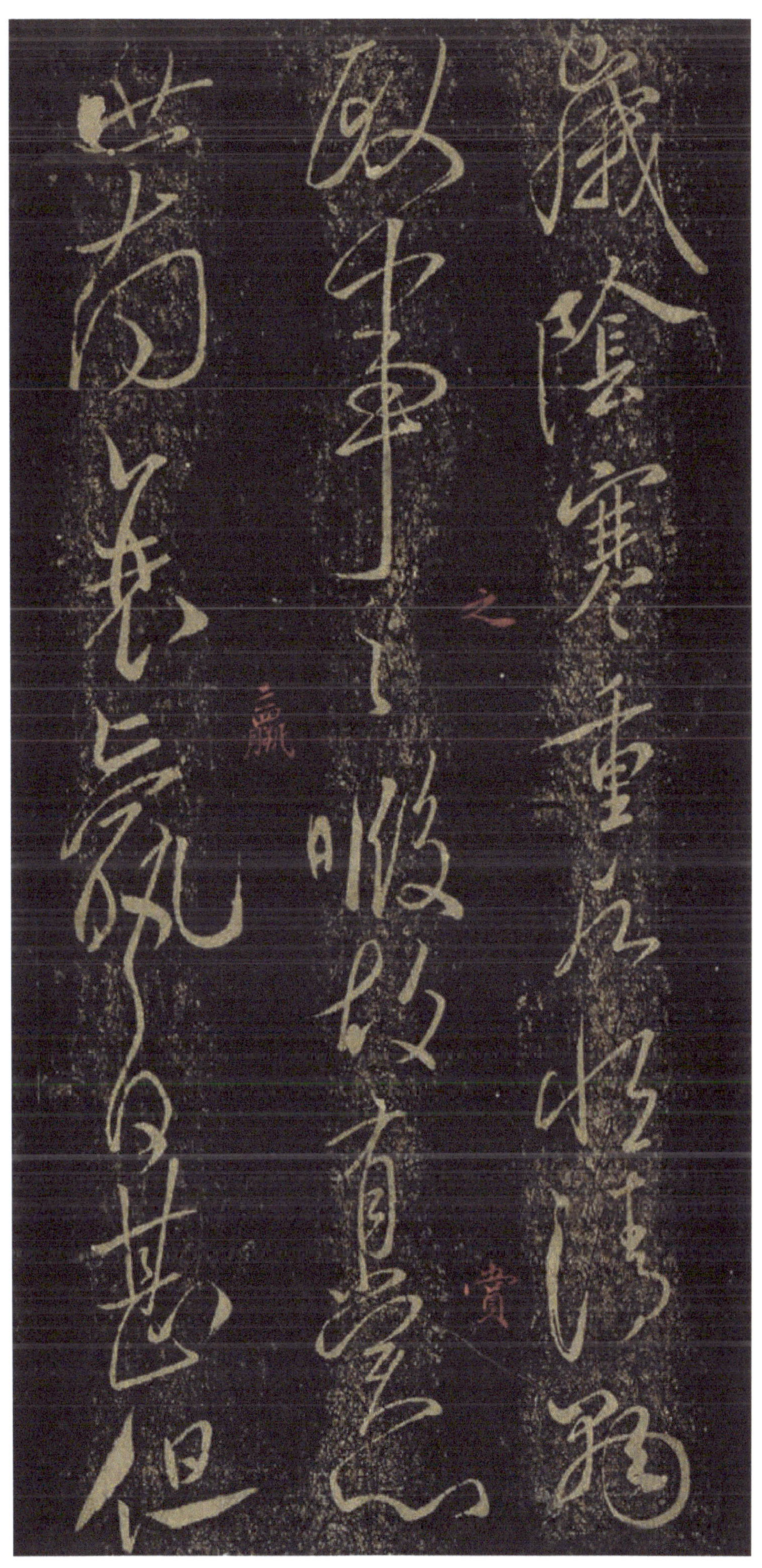

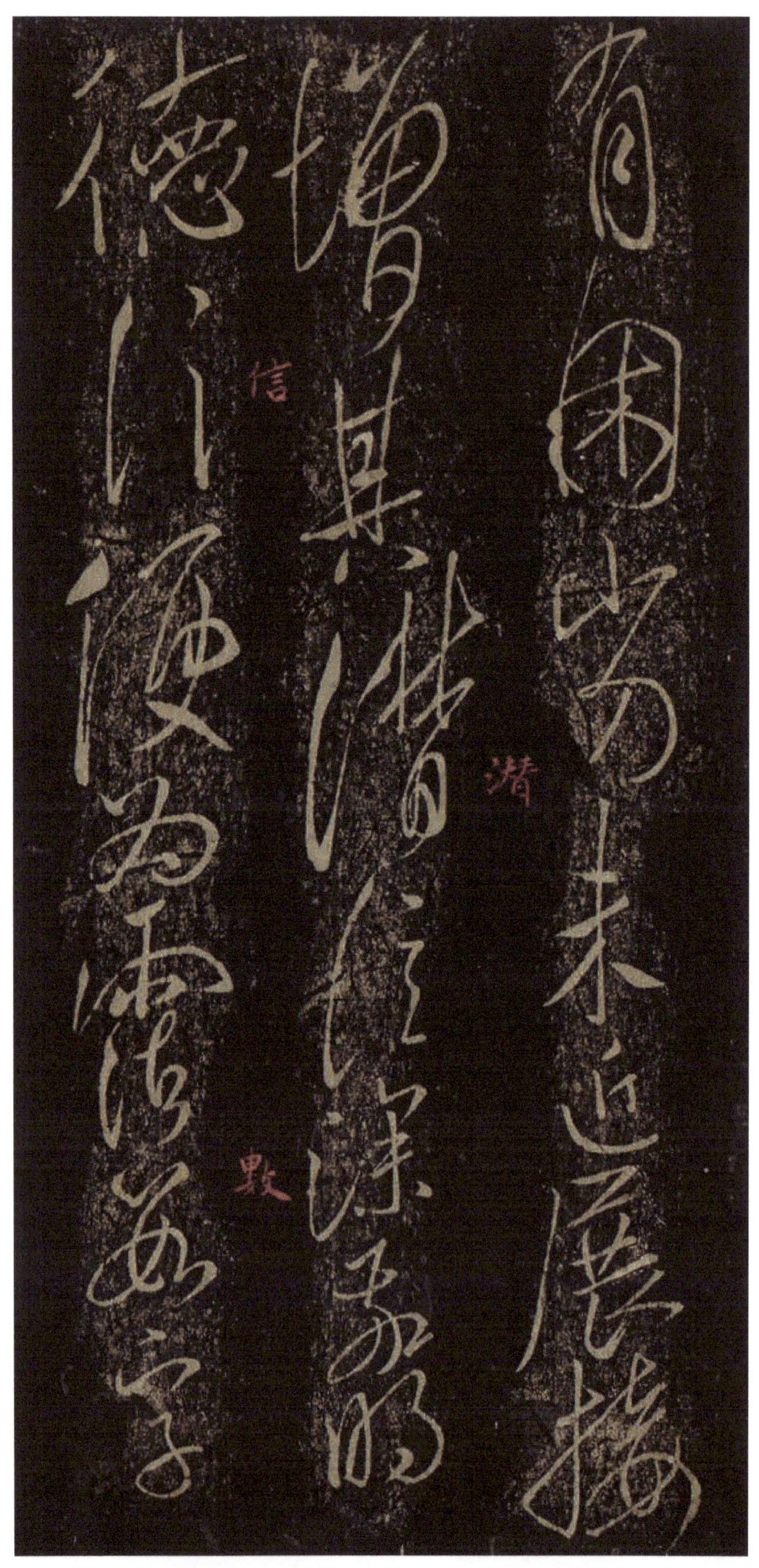
信
潜
敗

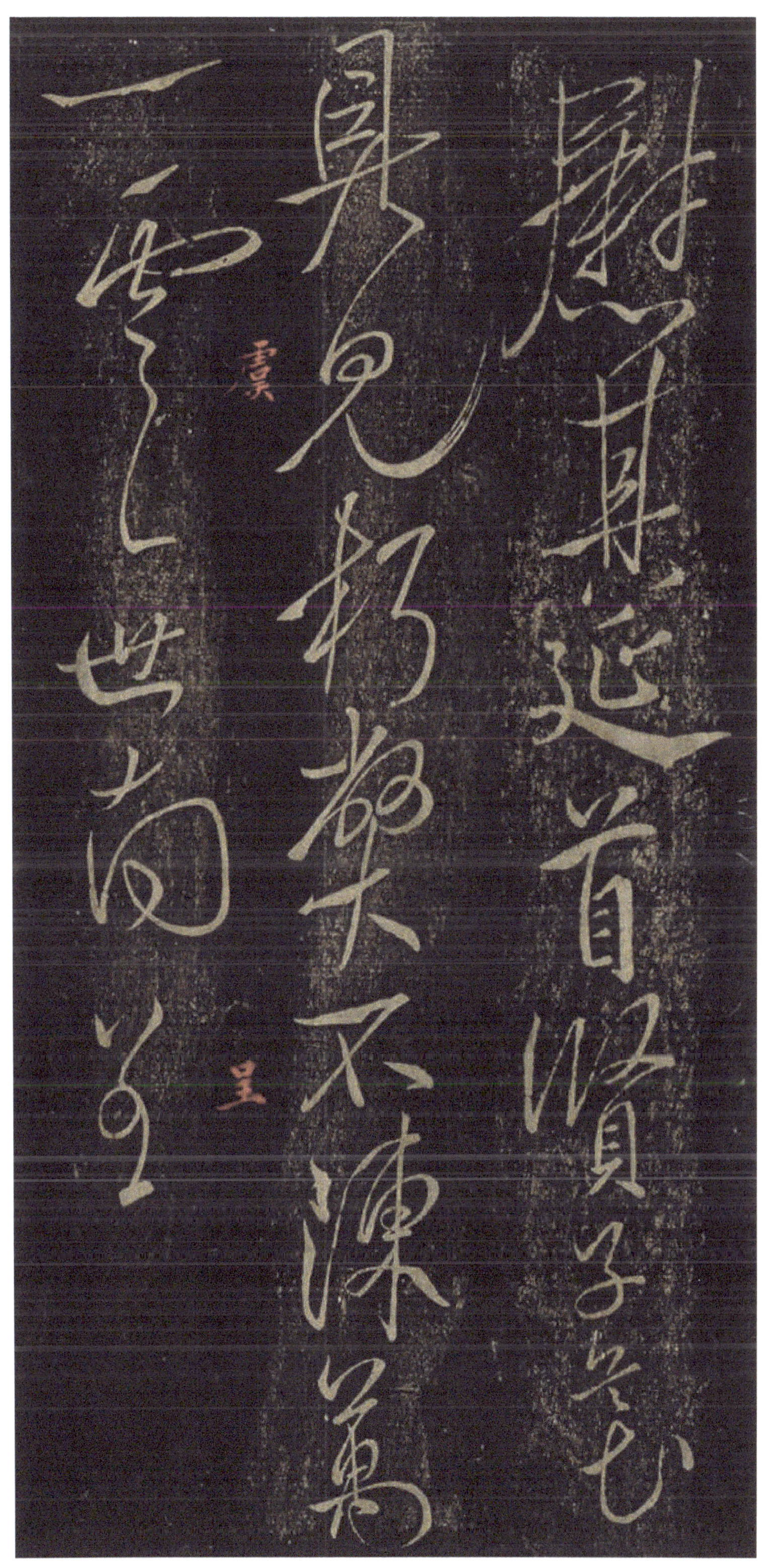

攀耳迤首以順子與心
梁見新奐不陳萬
一室世尚
雲
呈

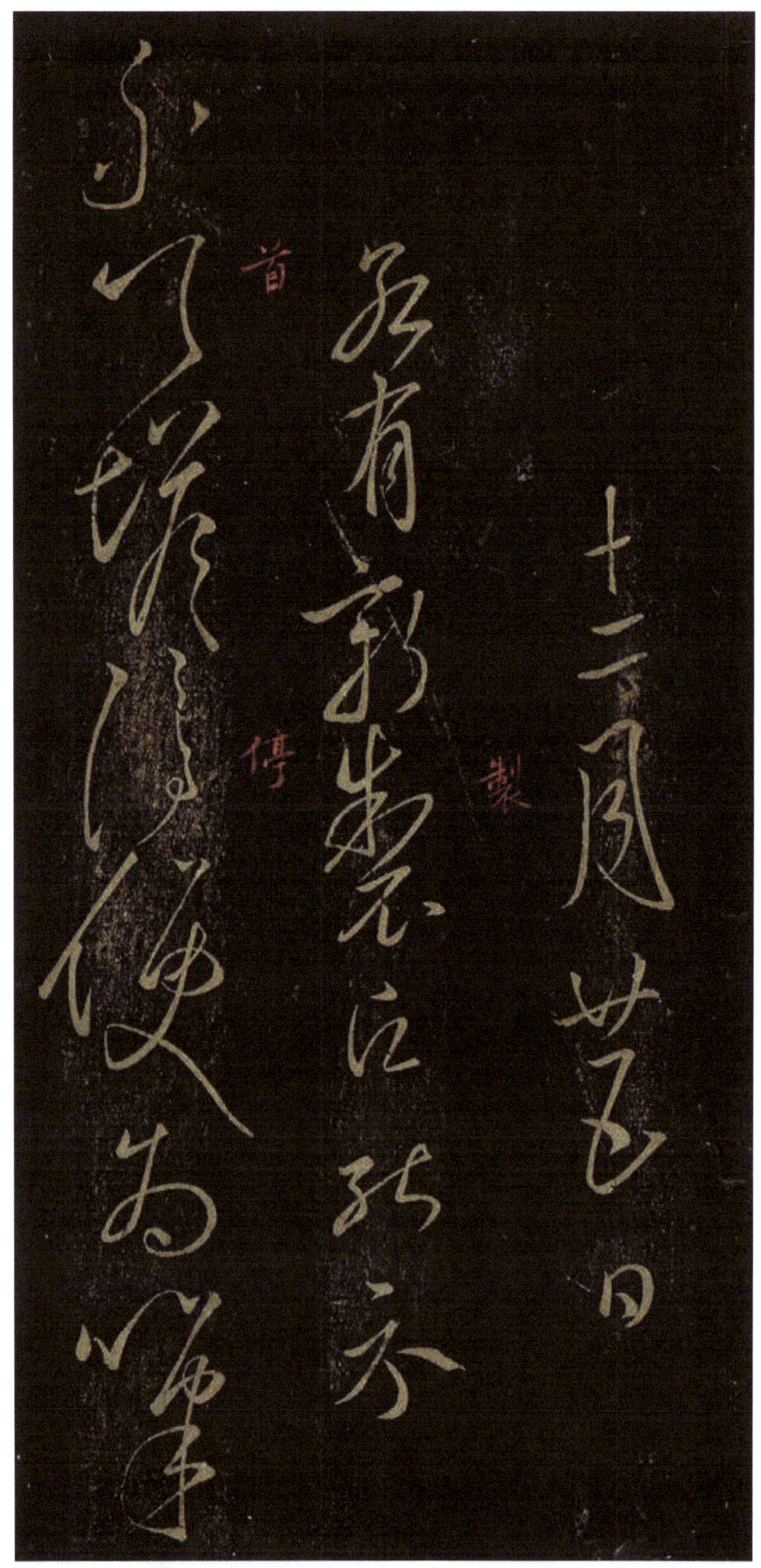

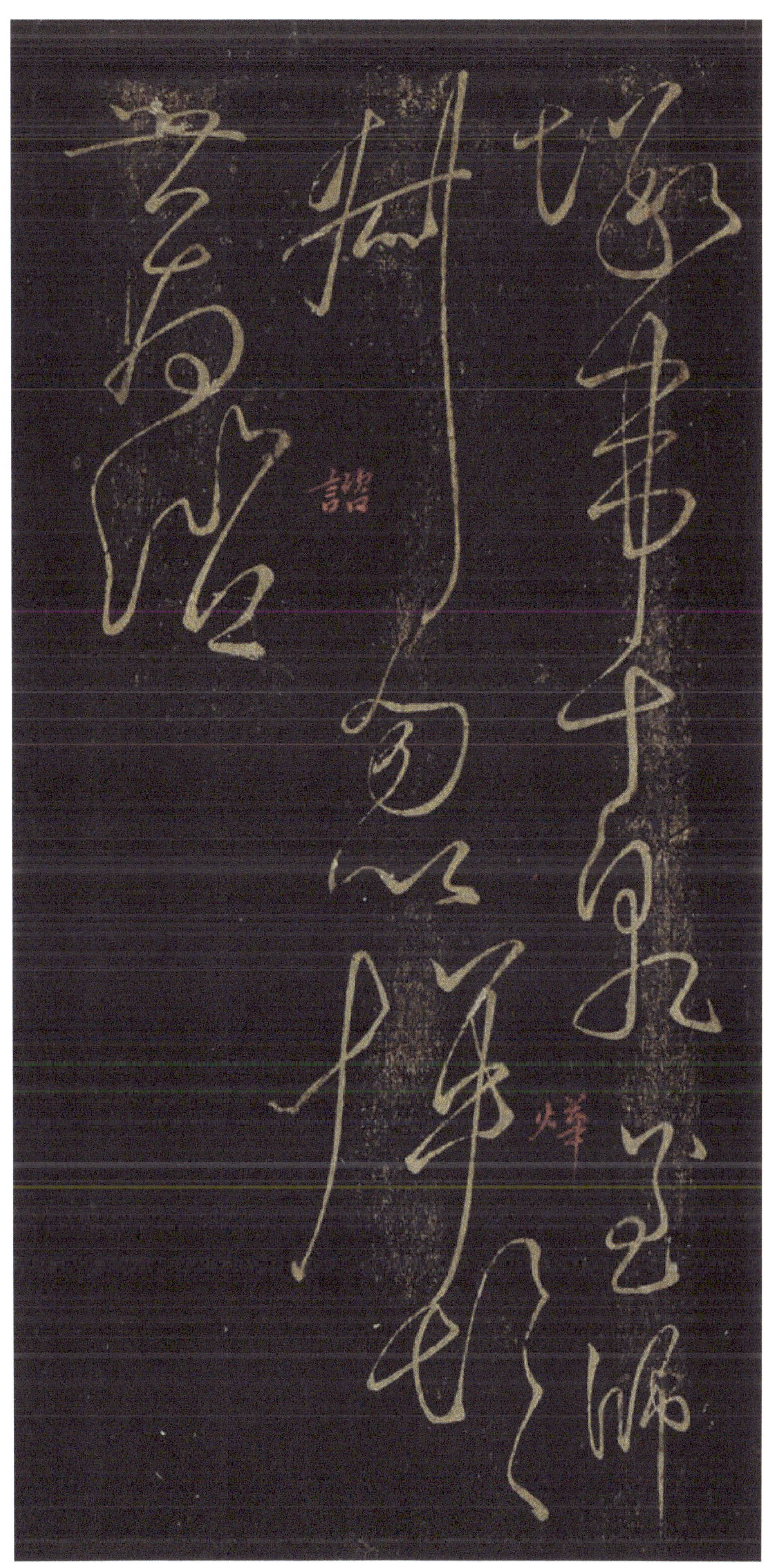

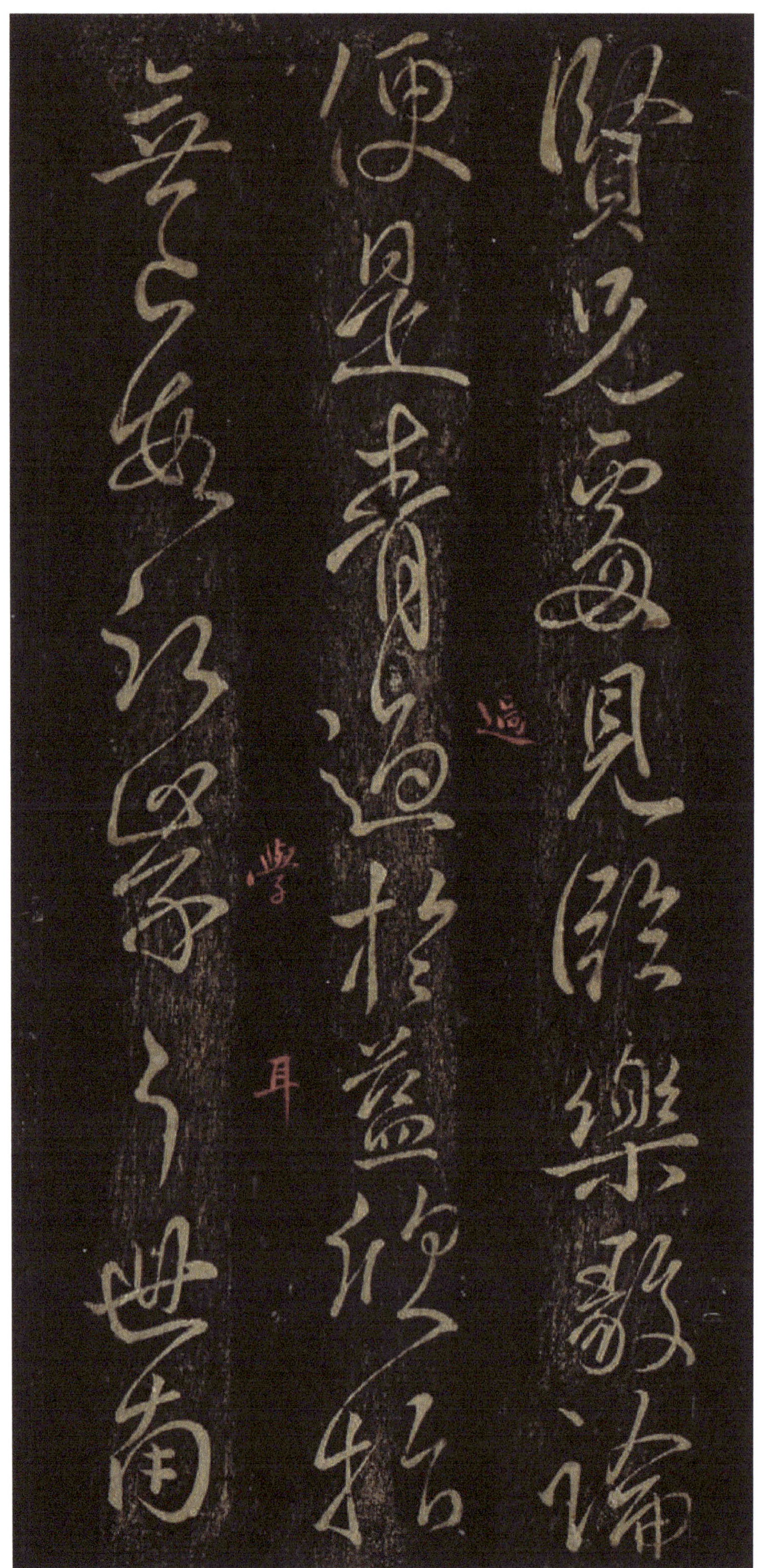

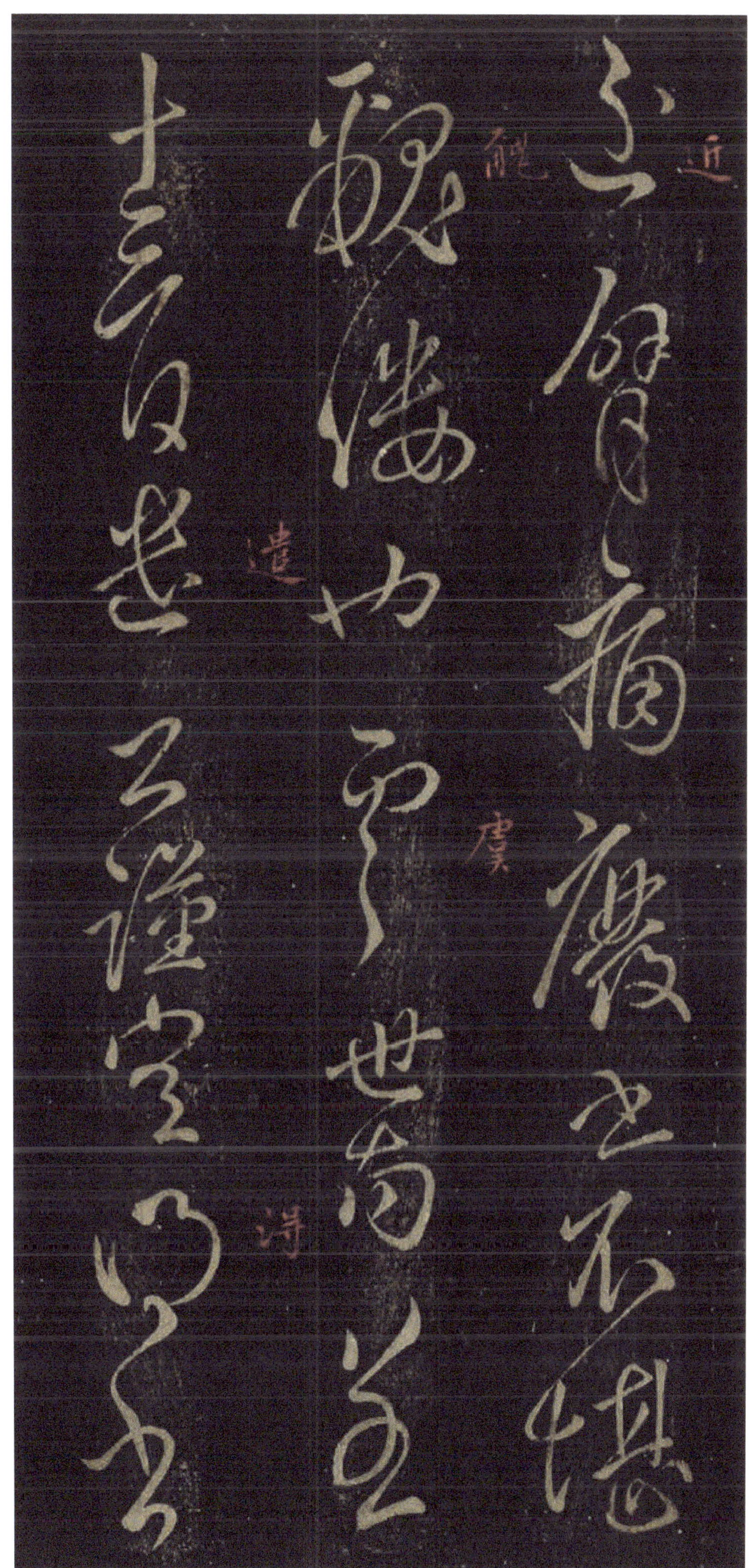

世南從去月廿七八十三字一尚　行

左脚更痛遂不朝會至今未

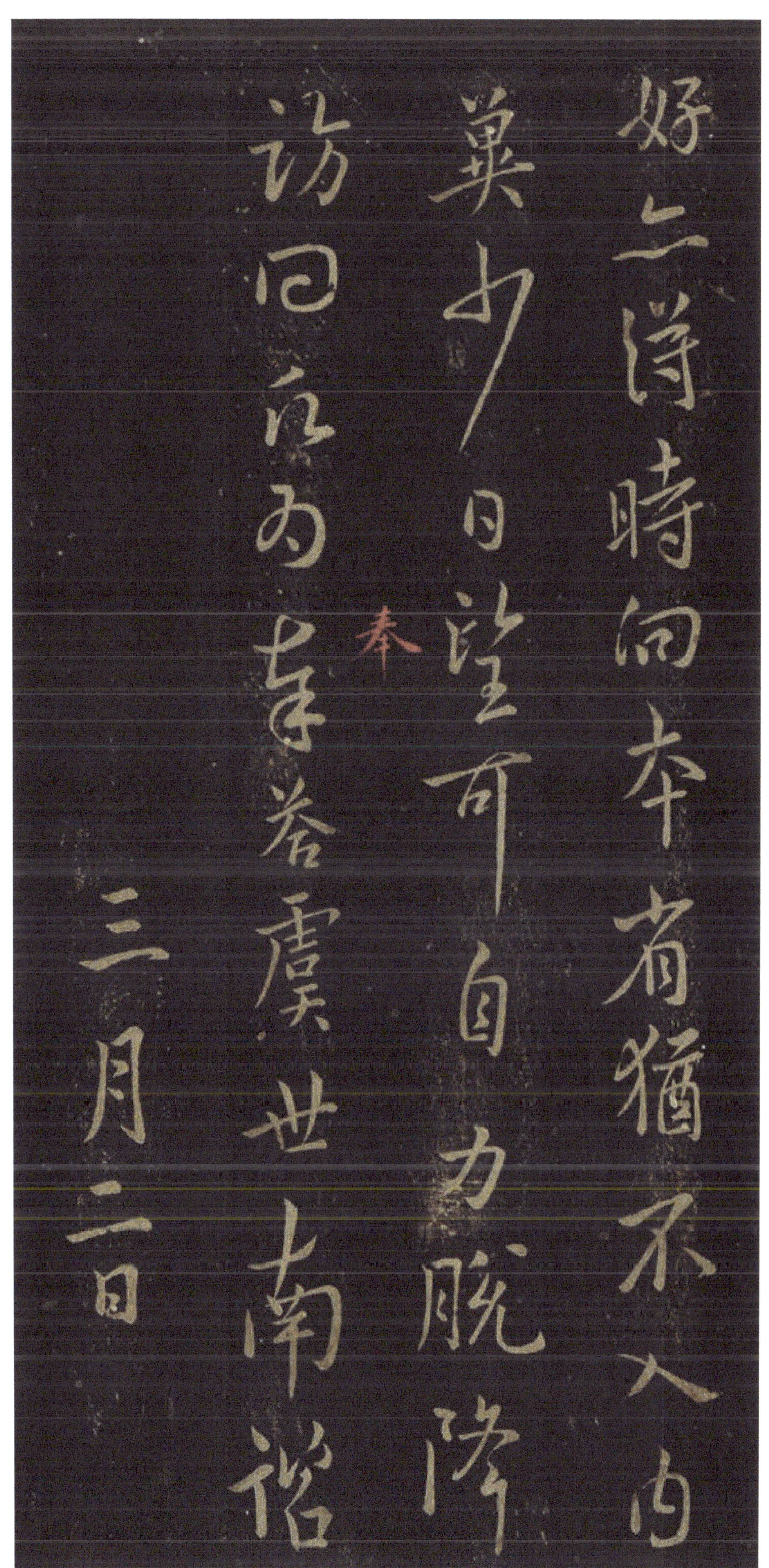

好二得時向本省猶入内
冀少日望可自力脫降
訪巳在南裕答虞世南
三月二日

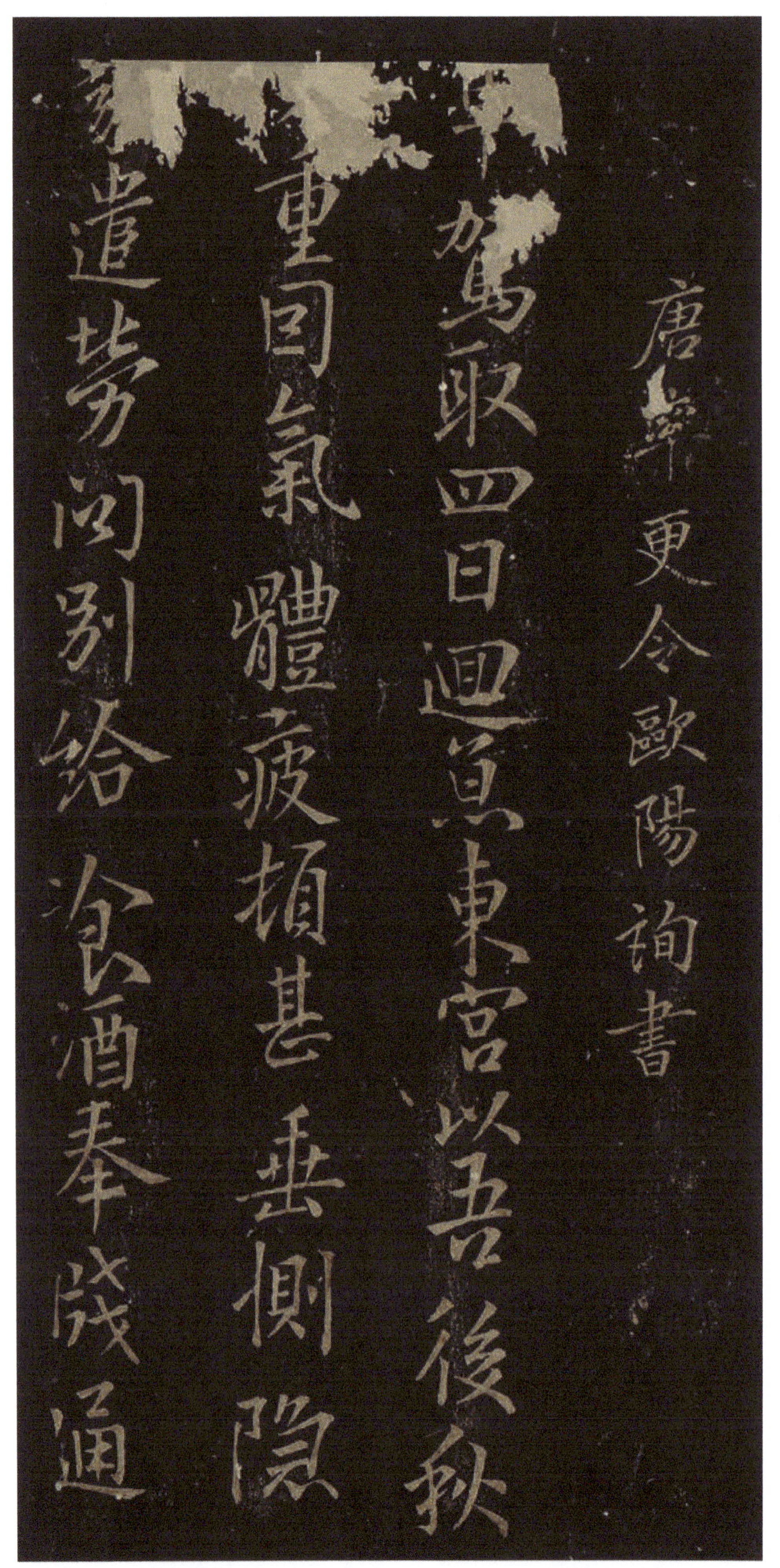

54

謝手命優、心愿欣荣崖㞗

嚴素弟恨此身已老盡忠所

特有平生之忘可惠子知我以絲

故云：賢壯並安佳詢再拜

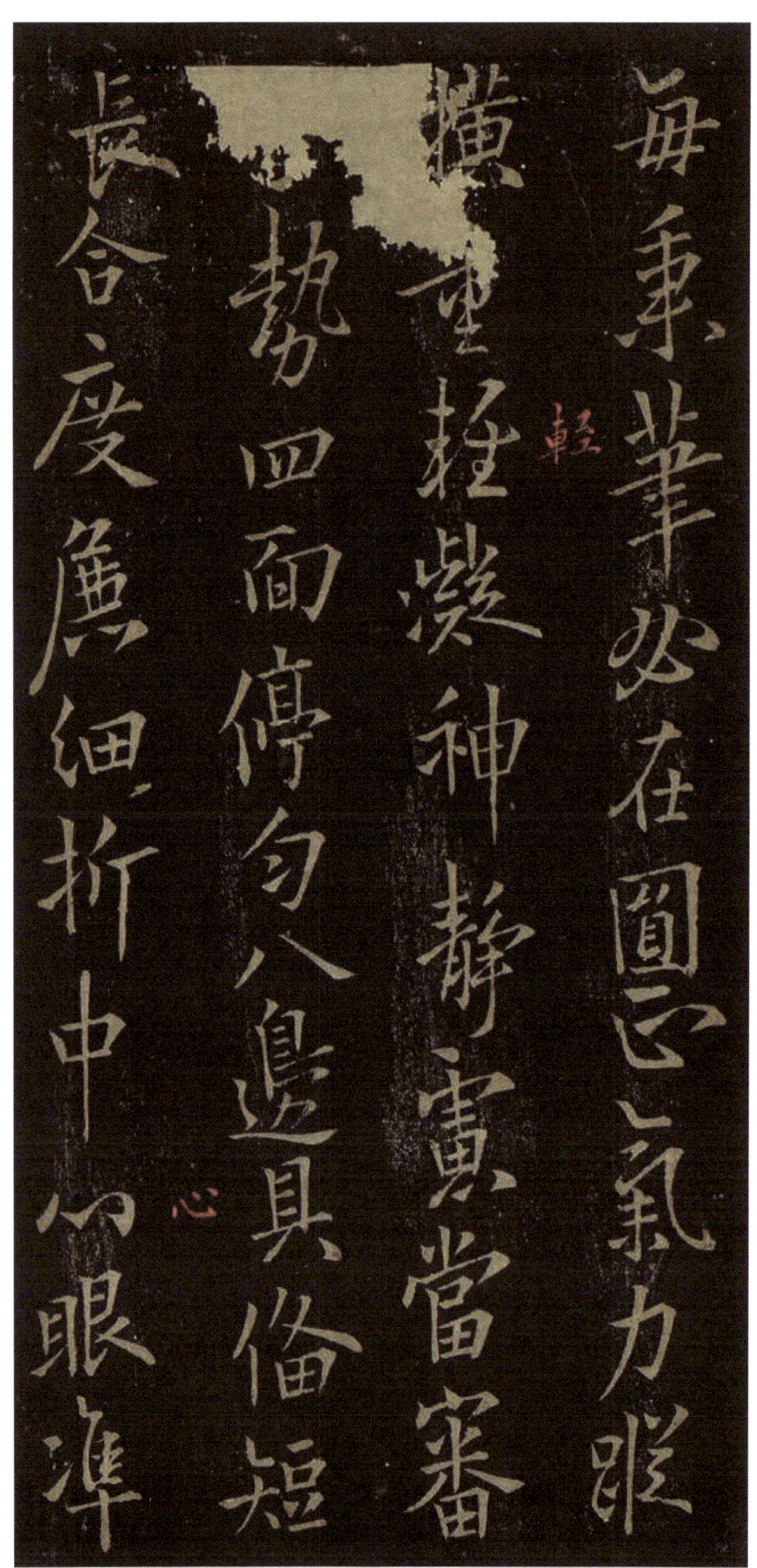

每秉筆必在圓正氣力
輕 凝神靜慮當審
勢四面停勻八邊具備短
長合度麤細折中心眼准

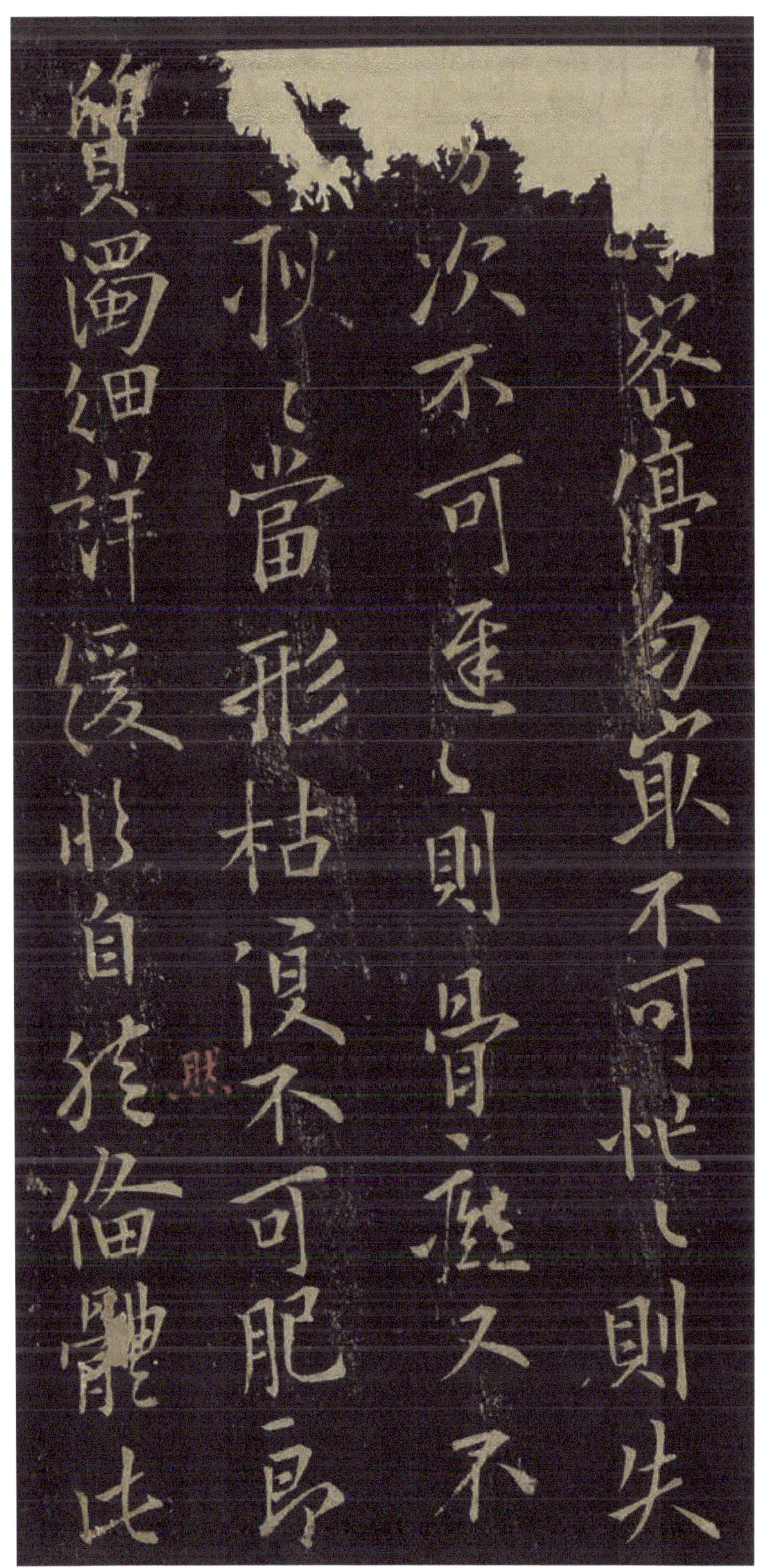
姿傳為軍不可忙則失
次不可遲則骨歷入不
秋之當形枯復不可肥身
貸濁細詳後附自然備體此

趙家冤妙裏付善奴轉授訣

觀六年七月十二日洵書

年守疾病無事絶心氣

書裏焉並昔時既言

必求然顯製字豈備矣

之十五日歐陽詢

九中得是下書知道體平

著氣力尚未結平復极欲

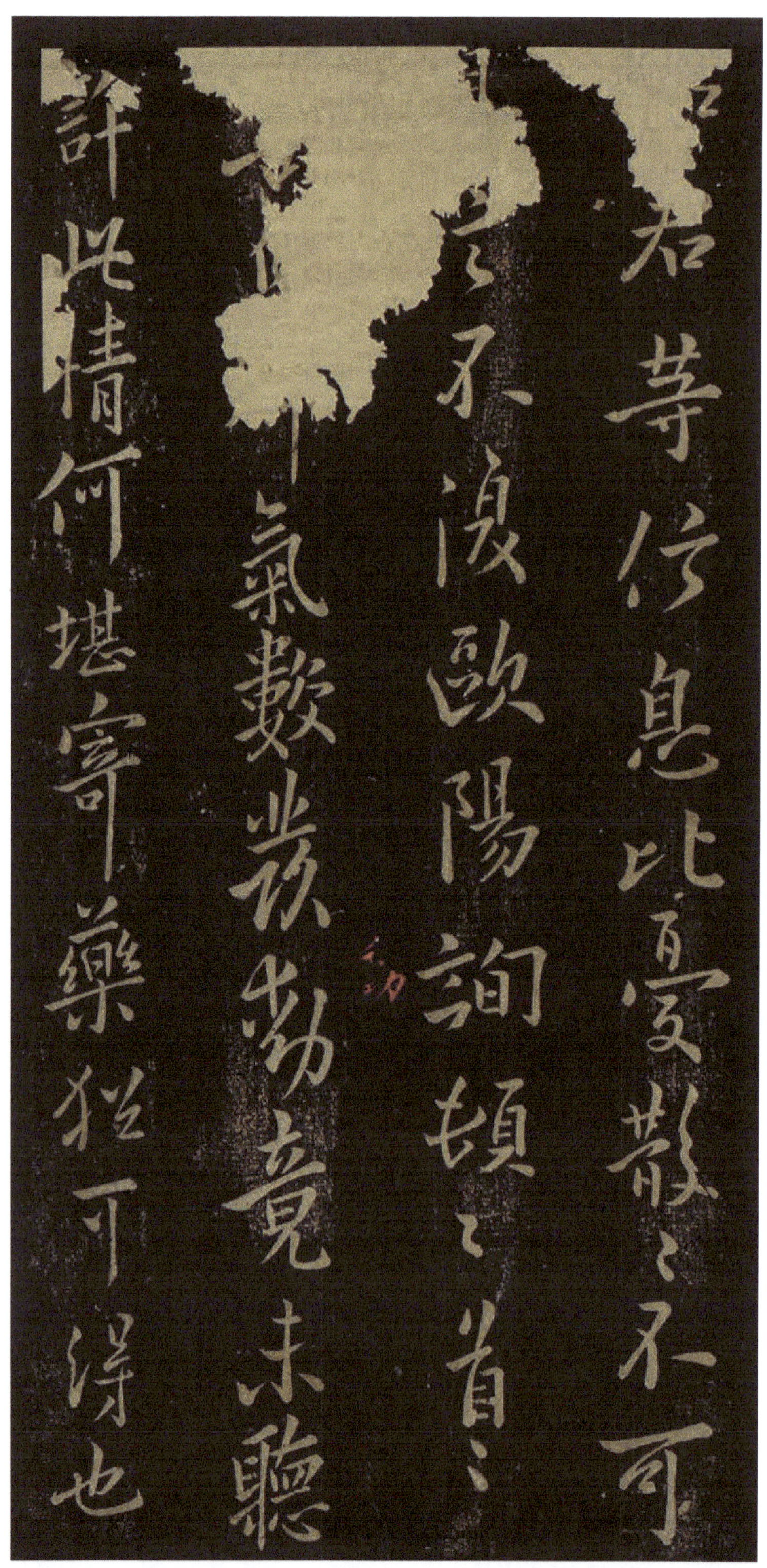

知葶竹息比受散之不可
之不復歐陽詢頓之省
氣數业劣竟未聽
許此情何堪寧寄藥猶可得也

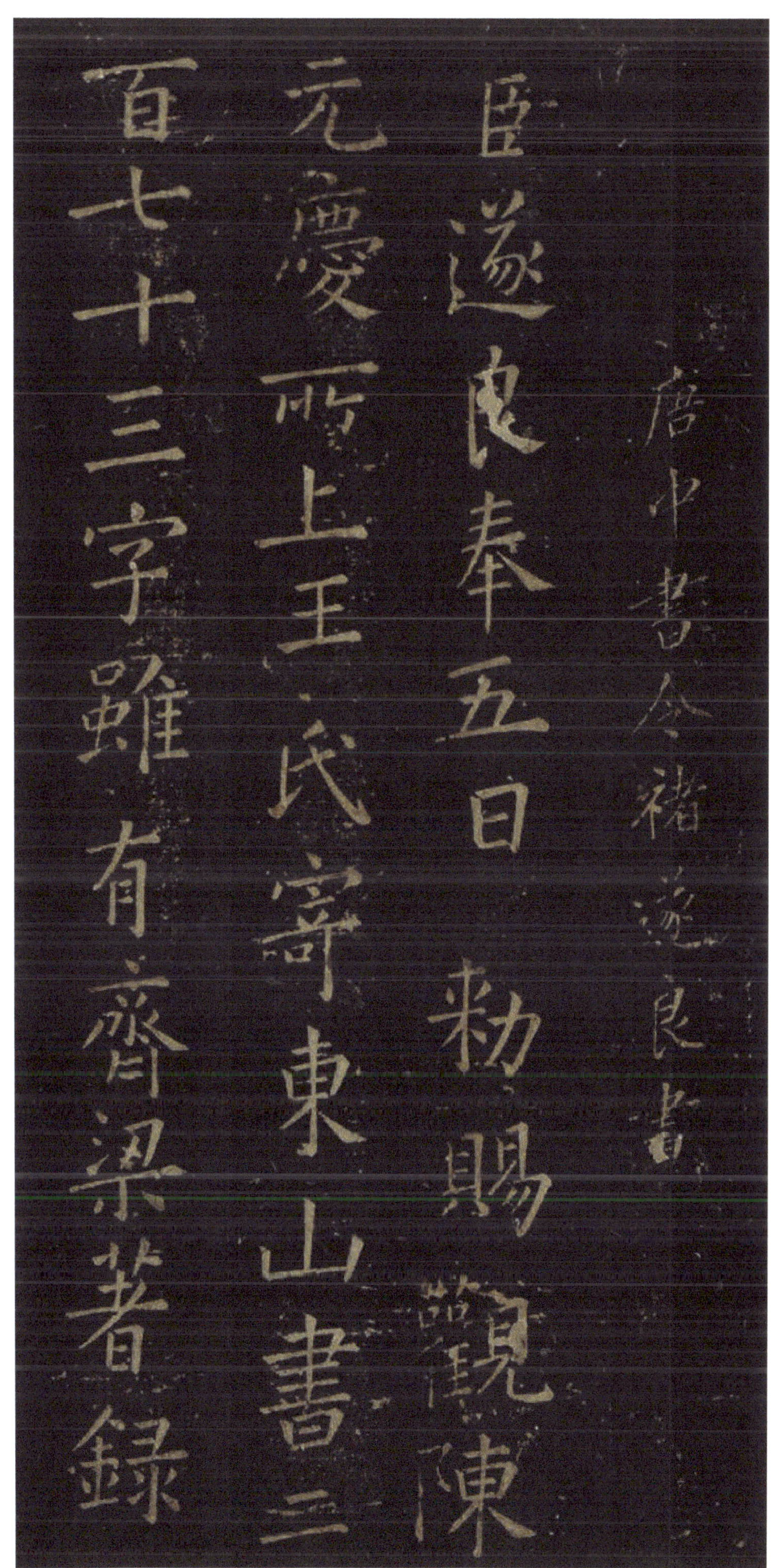

臣遂良奉五日勅賜觀陳

元慶而上王氏寧東山書三

百七十三字雖有齊梁著錄

唐中書令褚遂良書

而其年月不合盖安石太和
之元末歷中書王之去郡乃
永和末其非決矣且連城之
寶光景殊絕於武夫芝蘭

之苟豈蕭菌而可雜既經

聖覽寧侯臣言明恩不

遺辯列萬一侍書臣褚遂

良謹上

遂良頓首告六月八日報書

閑塗中侍奉安佳為尉

道妙近還至東歔氣體逆

还寧承与醫療已即平復除

深感慰遂良自南還已未

安悲首之争欵奉國恩

觸事成悲何可俞因高崖

二姪歸白此褚遂良再拜

家姪承法師道體安居深
為慰耳渡間久棄塵滓
與孫勤同龕一食清齋六時禪
誦得黑之果將与退轉也奉

洪水踰世載即日遂艮巘巘
盡白無復近歲之間要荒草
鸐雀之志餬餅悲且以
即日蒙恩驅使盡生報國隆

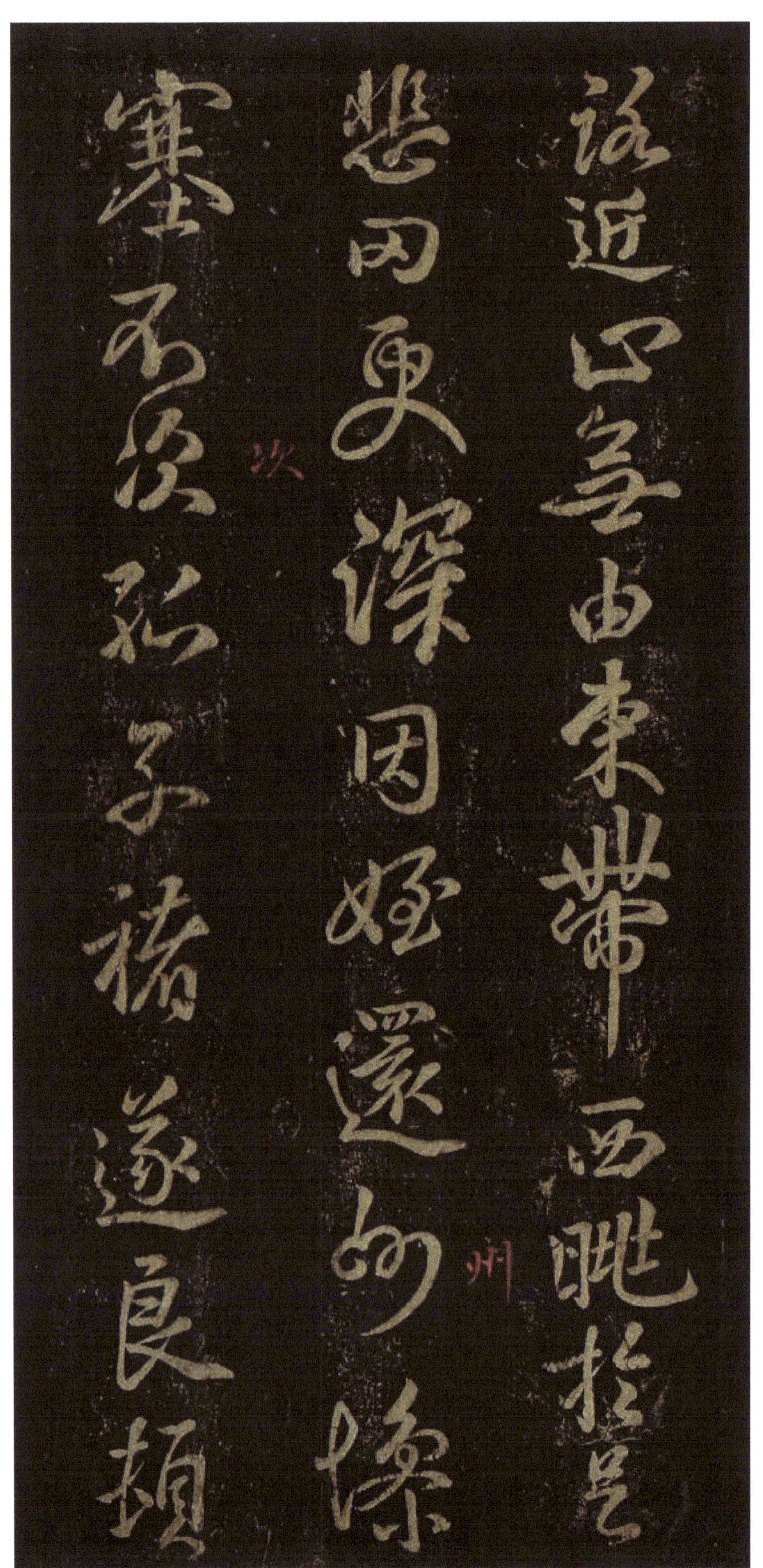

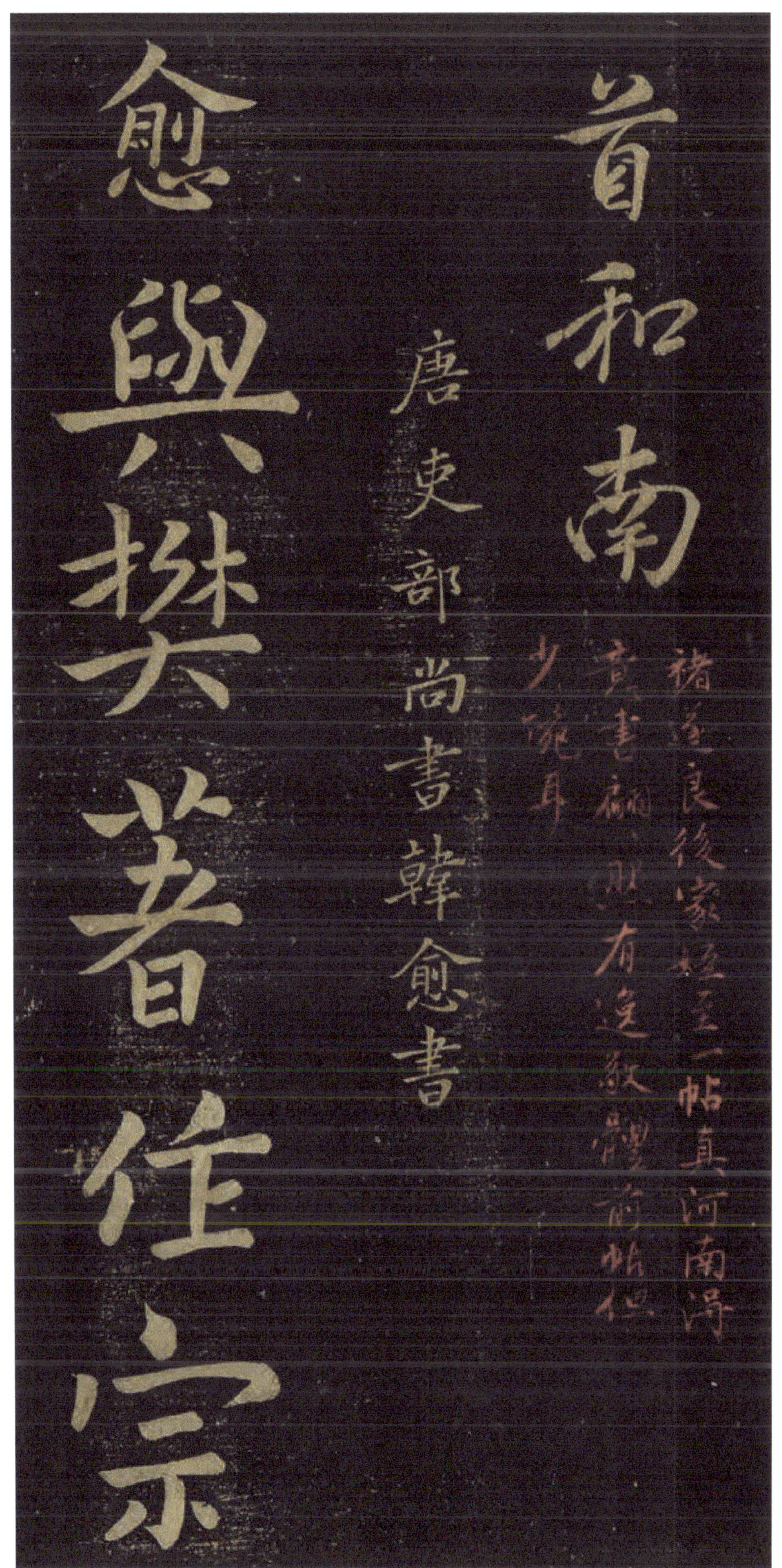

愈與樊著作宗
唐吏部尚書韓愈書
首和南
褚遂良後家趨至一帖真河南獨
少院耳
宣畫顒則有逵致體前帖但

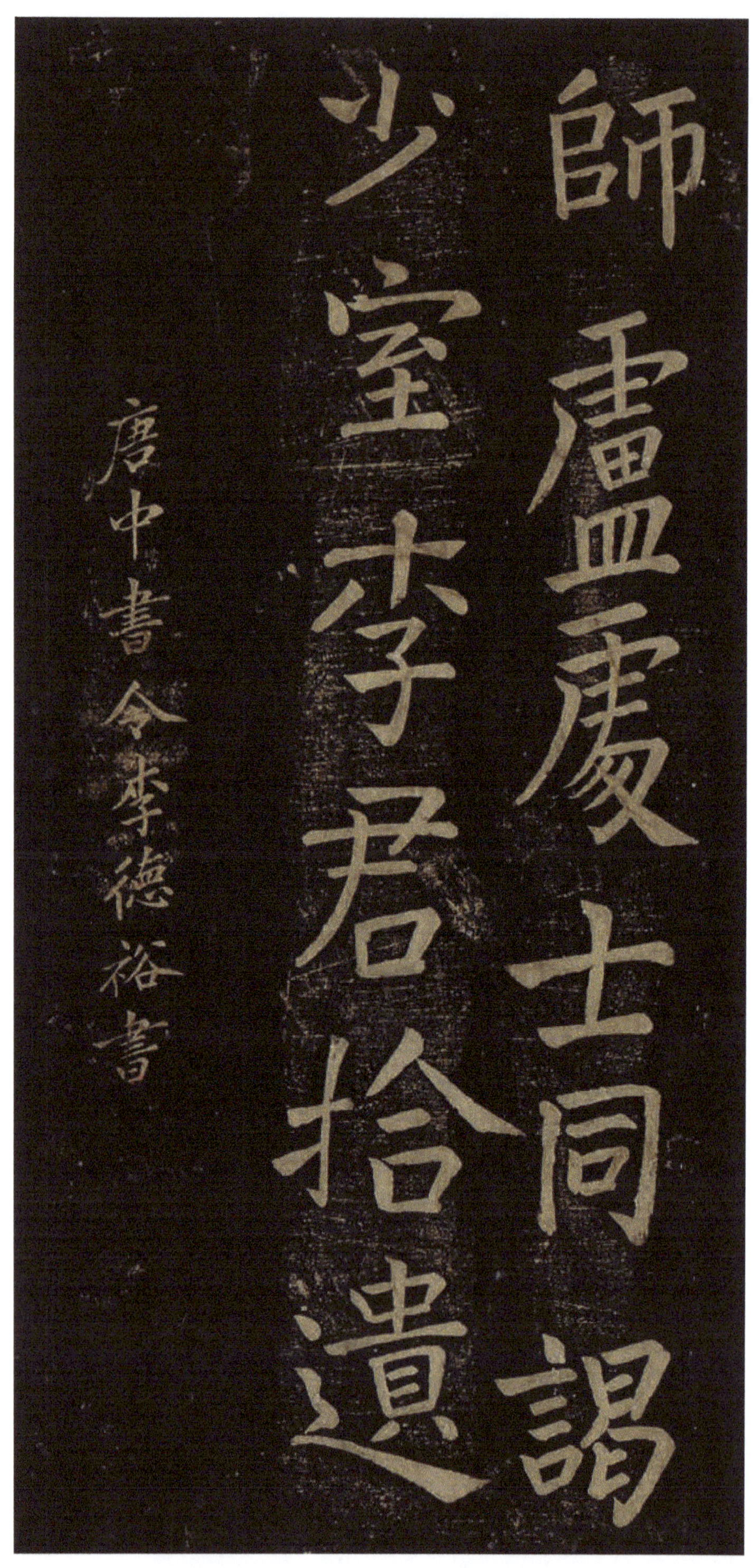
師盧慶士同謁
少室李君拾遺
唐中書令李德裕書

德裕

啟天地窮人物情所棄雖有骨

肉尔無音書平生舊知無復吊問

閣者至仁念舊盛德恤孤再降專

人遠途逾滇漲兼賜衣服器物茶藥

至多橋木暫榮寒灰稍暖開緘發

紙泝咽難勝大海之中無人枢恤資

鯰蕩盡家事一空百嗷然往、絶

食塊獨窮悴終日若飢雄恨垂殁

之年須作餞見之兜自十月末得疾伏
枕七旬其間屬纊者數四藥物陳
衰又無醫人妻命信天幸自活罷
備方其生意至微自料此生無咎

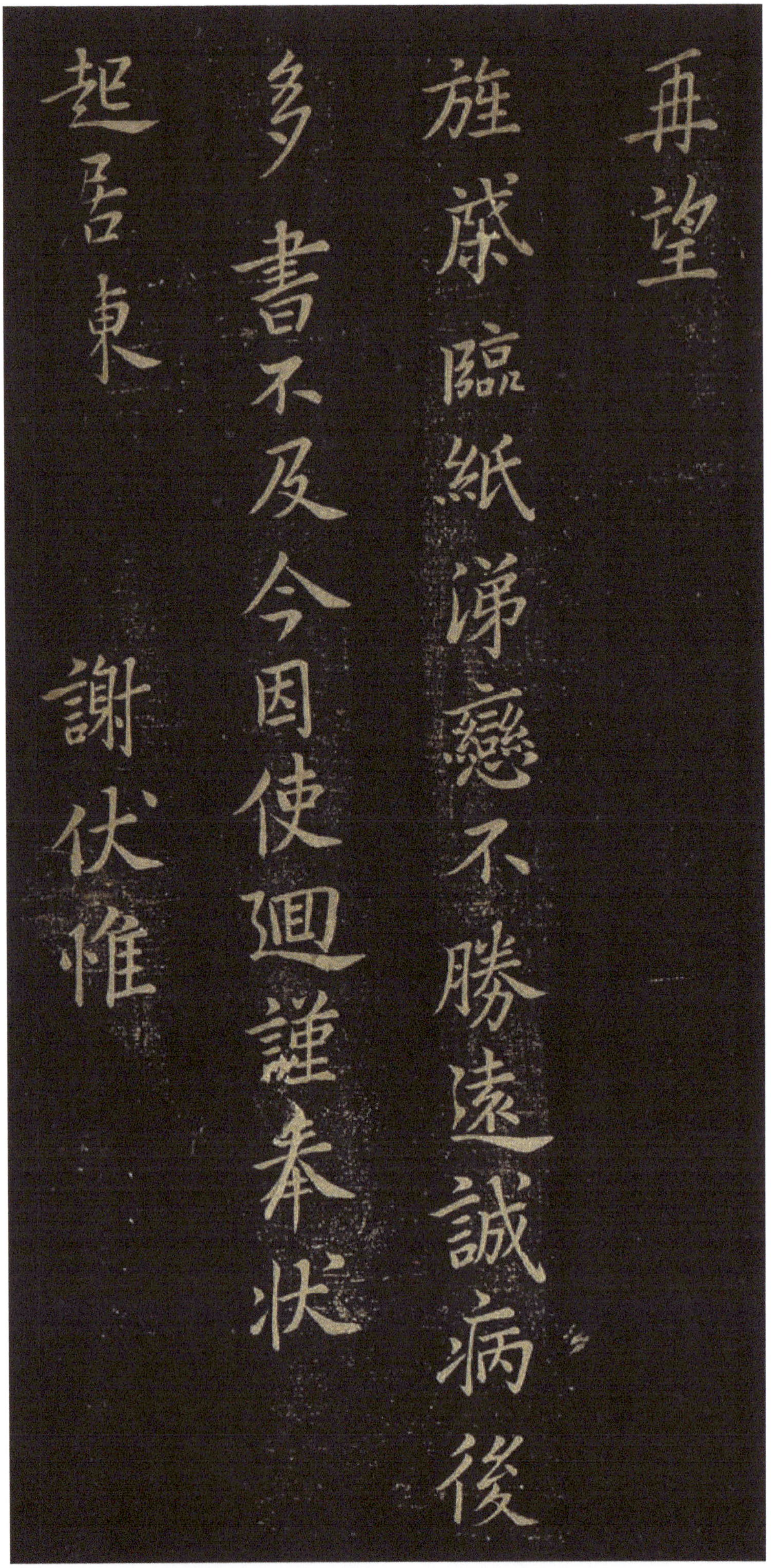

再望

旌麾臨紙涕戀不勝遠誠病後

多書不及今因使迴謹奉狀

謝伏惟

起居東

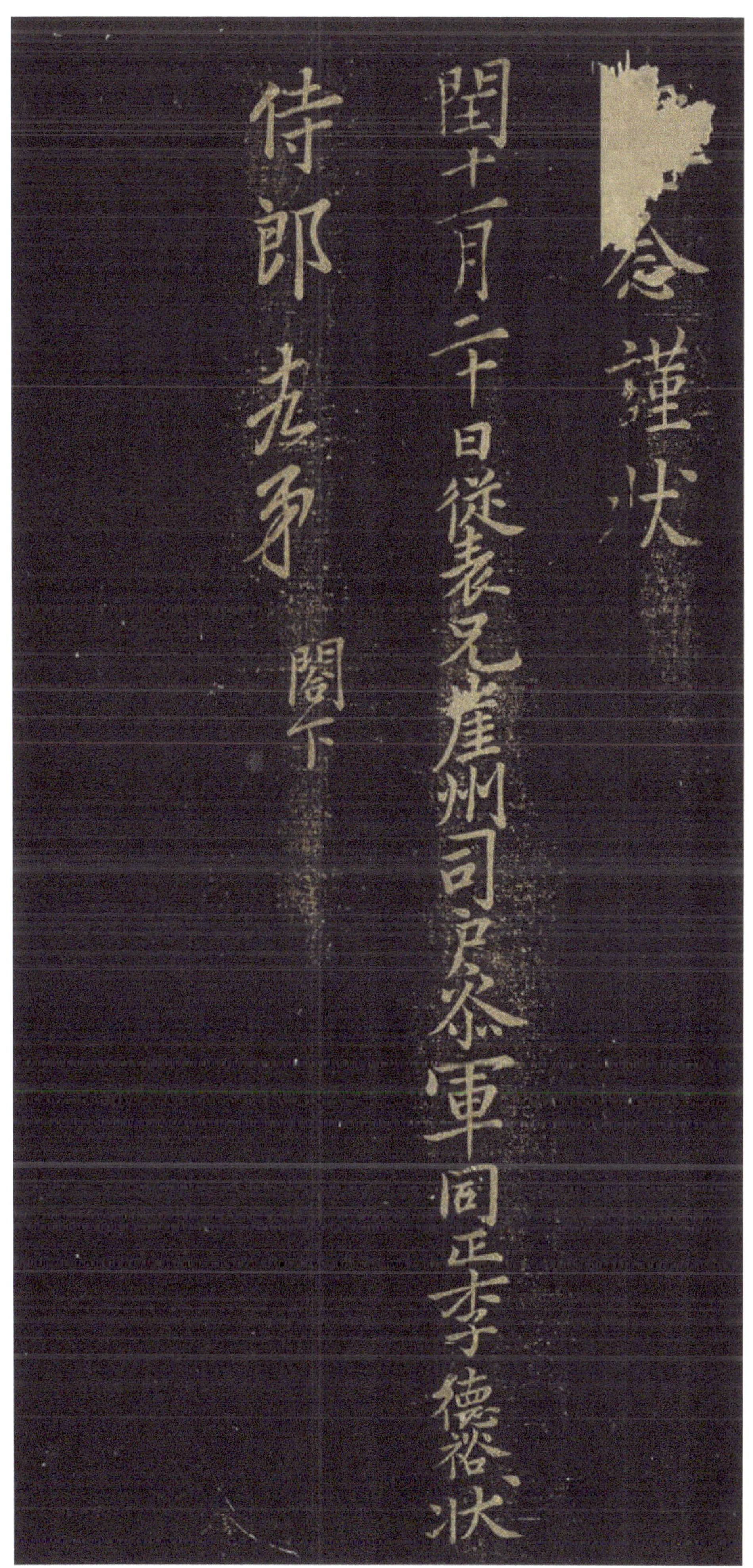
念

謹狀

閏十月二十日從表兄崖州司戶參軍同正李德裕狀

侍郎　老兄

閣下

一 晉禦史中丞劉環之書　環之頓首頓首　未陽遠感閏　知有患
耿耿　知
二 以自屈　恨不相見　力及不比望　環之
日賴郎翼頓首　節過多
三 □□書為慰　意以何如　深勞弊頓　曳力還不具　晉平北
將軍向秀書　　晉太守張冀書　□□
四 近聞華嶽有大崩石　奇□此不□□　知乎　故示
五 想定歇山不知　弟去不故令
六 晉平原內史陸機書　泰山高造
七 天峻極鬱　冥幽塗延
八 萬鬼神房　集白靈長
九 吟梁甫側　忼慷激楚
十 聲　晉司徒王珉書　十八日珉白　以二書暫至　未更
十一 近問　懸情不適　以可不　吾贏疾　故爾憂深　力書不具　王
珉敬問
十二 何如　僕故頓弊　力書不次　王珉頓首頓首　上下何如　僕
上下大都蒙恩　得書至之　吾雲今欲出耳　吾此月急遣　廿

十三 四是王濟祖日　欲必赴　卿可克克過　明吾友當下解相待
臨出亦遣報　既至王家畢　一可豫檄天公　令作一頓
十四 美食　可投其飯也　王前報　此年垂竟　悲懷
兼割　不自勝　奈何奈何　寒
十五 切體中此何似　甚耿耿　僕疾遂不差　眠食少　憂深　遣書
不次　王珉頓首頓首
十六 晉侍中王薈書　薈頓首　□□□□　為念　吾瘤腫甚□　甚
不次　王珉頓首
十七 □賴　力不具　□□頓首　晉侍中王操之書　操之等報白
承中書
十八 便　以安度永畢　念弟　追痛傷摧　哀恨絕不可
十九 堪　奈何　操之等報　操之等等　得識婢書　慰意　知年光數
問可不不得　蕫順
二十 消息懸心　操之頓首　晉司徒王廞書　告誘靜　媛靜
姝　此晦便當假葬　永痛抽剝　心情分割　不
二一 自勝　念汝等追痛摧慟　纏綿斷絕　何可堪任　痛當奈何
二二 當複奈何　遣悲涕不次　歔疏　晉黃門郎王渙之書
二三 渙之等白　不審二嫂常患複何如　馳情　倫直等平安　計嫂

倫奴已應在道 企遲 適東五日 動靜最差 速

佳渙之等白 **晉丞相王導書**

二三 姑如複小勝 冀遂和耳 猶不寧 餘上下故常患反側 此悉

二四 省示具卿 辛酸之至 吾甚憂勞 卿此事亦不蹔忘 然書

二五 足下所欲致身處尚在轂中 王制正自欲不得許 卿當

二六 如何 導亦天明往 導白 改朔情增傷感

二七 濕惡 自何如 頗小覺損不帖有應不懸耿速哀勞滿所 不

具 王

二八 導 **晉司徒王殉書** 珣頓首頓首 伯遠勝業情

二九 期群從之寶 自以羸患 志在優遊 始獲此出意不克申 心

別如昨永為疇

三十 古 遠隔嶺嶠 不相瞻臨 三月四日珣頓首 末冬眾感 得

七月書 知問寒 何

三一 如 秋槃憂之劣不具 王珣頓首白 **晉司徒王蒙書**

三二 蒙死罪前亦比得諸葛餘抗書及此義 故誠宜敦率 然其去

此縣 近十年 經歷四五長吏矣 欲斂其時吏 則十無一在 欲調

民則不知以

三三 何為辭 且諸葛僕財之弟始 去餘杭以情料之當非至困者

願便以下官餞答之 謹白 蒙死罪 **晉中書令王洽書**

三四 洽白 辱告承問 洽故爾劣劣 冀以複敘 還白不具 王洽

再拜 洽頓首言 不孝禍深 備豫嬰荼

三五 毒 蔭恃亡兄仁愛之訓 冀終百年永有憑奉 何圖慈兄一

旦背棄 悲號哀摧 肝心如抽 痛毒煩冤 不自堪忍 酷當奈何

三六 至 感增斷絕 執筆哽涕 不知所言 洽頓首言 洽頓首言

兄子號毀 不可忍視之摧心 發言哽慟 當複奈何奈何

三七 洽頓首言洽白 向感塞不成敘 得告承問 殊乏劣 白不具

王洽再拜 **晉侍中王彪書**

三八 得仁祖廿一日示 知侍巾已還 廣複四月必來居此 足下

為至 視之 **晉黃門郎王徽之書**

三九 二日 告□氏女 新月哀摧不自勝 奈何奈何 念痛慕 不

可任 得疏知汝故異惡懸心 雨濕熱複何似 食不 吾牽勞並頓

勿複 數日還

四十 汝比自護 力不具 徽之等書 姚懷珫 滿騫

四一　唐工部尚書狄仁傑書　孟冬漸寒伏惟　尊體起　萬福　仁
傑即　蒙
四二　恩不審近日　寢膳何似　自成　違間　將及半年　每屬縈仍
曾無一劄　惶悚之外　攀戀實深　人使遠來　□翰猥至　□
四三　捧欣佩　交集下懷　兼有□霑　出於紀念　未期□高會　企
望增深　使回奉狀□起居陳謝　不宣　謹狀
四四　十月□日從表弟地官侍郎判尚書同鳳閣鸞臺平章事狄仁
傑狀　唐秘書少監虞世南書　積時傾心　非翰墨所具
四五　歲陰寒重　願恒清朝　政事之遐　故有賞心　世南衰羸日甚
但
四六　有困劣　未近展接　增其潛泣　深敬明德　信便為霑數字
四七　慰其延首　賢子書具見　朽弊不陳萬一　虞世南呈
四八　十二月廿五日　若有新制　願能示　不行憺停便為歎
四九　塚事　十幹至師叔　勿以憐煩　世南諮
五十　賢兄處見臨樂毅論　便是青過於藍　欣指無已　數願學耳
世南
五一　近臂痛　廢書不堪　觀縷也　虞世南呈　十三日遣公　謹定
得書

五二　為慰　可言也　世南從去月廿七八　率一曹行　左腳更痛
遂不朝會　至今未
五三　好　亦得時向本省　猶不入內　冀少日望可自力　脫降訪問
願為奉答　虞世南諮　三月二日
五四　唐率更令歐陽詢書　□駕取四日回京　東宮以吾後秋□重
因　氣體疲頓　甚垂惻隱　□遣勞問　別給餐酒　奉賤通
五五　謝　手命優□　□恐欣榮　豈任誠素　弟恨此身已老　盡忠
所特□平生之心耳　惠子知我　茲故云云　賢淑並安佳　詢再拜
五六　每秉筆必在圓正　氣力縱橫　重輕凝神　靜慮當審　□勢四
面停均　八邊俱備　短長合度　麤細折中　心眼准
五七　□　□密停勻　最不可忙　忙則失□　次不可遲　遲則骨癡
又不□瘦　瘦當形枯　複不可肥　肥即質濁　細詳緩臨　自然備體
此
五八　是最要妙處　付善奴轉授訣　□觀六年七月十二日　詢書
五九　必求　然顯數字　豈能備矣　□□□之十五日　歐陽詢
□年守疾病　無事絕心氣　□□書處焉　並昔時既言
六十　知君等資訊　比憂散　散不可　□□不復　歐陽詢頓首頓首
中得足下書　知道體平□　□□氣力尚未能平復　極欲

□□□氣數發動　竟未聽許　此情何堪　寄藥　猶可得也

六一　**唐中書令褚遂良書**　臣遂良奉五日敕　賜觀陳元慶所上

王氏寄東山書二百七十三字　雖有齊梁著錄

六二　而其年月不合　蓋安石太和之元　未曆中書　王之去郡　乃

永和末　其非決矣　且連城之寶　光景殊絕　於武夫芝蘭

六三　之芳　豈蕭菌而可雜　既經聖覽　寧俟臣言　明恩不遺辯列

萬一　侍書臣褚遂良謹上

六四　遂良頓首　得六月八日報書　聞塗中侍奉安佳　為慰　道州

近還至東畿　氣體小不寧　承與醫療　療即平復　彌

六五　深感尉　遂良自南遷已未　每思白首之年　孤奉國恩　觸事

成悲　何言可喻　因高崔二侄歸白此　褚遂良再拜

六六　家侄至　承法師道體安居　深以為慰耳　複聞久棄塵滓　與

彌勒同龕　一食清齋　亦時禪誦　得果已來　將無退轉也　奉別

六七　倏爾逾卅載　即日　遂良須鬢盡白　兼複近歲之間　嬰茲草

甚　燕雀之志　觸緒生悲　且以即日蒙恩驅使　盡生報國　途

六八　路近止無由東帶　西眺於足悲罔更深　因侄還州　慘塞不次

孤子諸遂良頓

六九　首和南　**唐吏部尚書韓愈書**　愈與樊著作宗

七十　師盧處士全謁少室李君拾遺　**唐中書令李德裕書**

七一　德裕啟天地窮人　物情所棄　雖有骨肉　亦無音書　平生舊

知　無複吊問

閣老至仁念舊　盛德恤孤　冉降專人　遠逾溟漲　兼賜衣服　器物

茶藥

七二　至多　槁木暫榮　寒灰稍暖　閉緘發□□　咽難勝　大海之中

無人拯恤　資儲蕩盡　家事一空　百口嗷然　往往絕食　塊獨窮悴

終日若饑　唯恨垂歿

七三　之年　須作餒兒之鬼　自十月末得疾伏枕七旬　其間屬纊者

數四　藥物陳□又無醫人　委命信天　幸自活　羸憊方其　生意至

微　自料此生　無由

七四　再望旌棨　臨紙涕戀　不勝遠誠　病後多書不及　今因使回

謹奉狀　起居陳　謝伏惟

七五　□念謹狀　閏十一月二十日從表兄崖州司戶參軍同正李

德裕狀

侍郎十九弟　閣下